The Effective Teacher's Guide to Dyslexia and Other Learning Difficulties (Learning Disabilities)

This highly anticipated second edition of *The Effective Teacher's Guide to Dyslexia and Other Learning Difficulties (Learning Disabilities)* critically examines the specificity and complexity of learning disabilities. This user-friendly text highlights the importance of schools reviewing their curricula and assessment, pedagogical methods, resources, organisation and therapy procedures to ensure that their provision helps encourage academic progress and the best personal and social development for their pupils.

This book accessibly and authoritatively addresses a range of issues associated with:

- reading disorder/dyslexia
- disorder of written expression/dysgraphia
- developmental co-ordination disorder/dyspraxia
- mathematics disorder/dyscalculia.

Offering what works in the classroom, this text also takes into account the relationship between professionals who work closely with parents and other professionals. It helpfully recognises the importance of professional contributions and the foundational disciplines that contribute to special education. Underpinned by research and widely held professional opinions, this second edition of *The Effective Teacher's Guide to Dyslexia and Other Learning Difficulties (Learning Disabilities)* will prove a practical, readable and invaluable resource for busy teachers, students on initial teacher training courses and school managers and administrators.

Michael Farrell is a widely published private special education consultant. He works with children, families, schools, local authorities, voluntary organisations, published books extensiv he Special Education Han

D1329327

The Effective Teacher's Guides Series, all by Michael Farrell

The Effective Teacher's Guide to Behavioural and Emotional Disorders: Disruptive behaviour disorders, anxiety disorders and depressive disorders, and attention deficit hyperactivity disorder, 2nd edition
PB: 978-0-415-56568-4 (Published 2010)

The Effective Teacher's Guide to Sensory and Physical Impairments: Sensory, orthopaedic, motor and health impairments, and traumatic brain injury, 2nd edition
PB: 978-0-415-56565-3 (Published 2010)

The Effective Teacher's Guide to Autism and Communication Difficulties, 2nd edition
PB: 978-0-415-69383-7 (Published 2012)

The Effective Teacher's Guide to Dyslexia and Other Learning Difficulties (Learning Disabilities), 2nd edition
PB: 978-0-415-69385-1 (Published 2012)

The Effective Teacher's Guide to Moderate, Severe and Profound Learning Difficulties (Cognitive Impairments), 2nd edition
PB: 978-0-415-69387-5 (Published 2012)

The Effective Teacher's Guide to Dyslexia and Other Learning Difficulties (Learning Disabilities)

Practical strategies

Second edition

Michael Farrell

Routledge
Taylor & Francis Group

LONDON AND NEW YORK

First published 2006 by Routledge
This second edition published 2012
by Routledge
2 Park Square, Milton Park, Abingdon, Oxon OX14 4RN

Simultaneously published in the USA and Canada
by Routledge
711 Third Avenue, New York, NY 10017

Routledge is an imprint of the Taylor & Francis Group, an informa business

British Library Cataloguing in Publication Data
A catalogue record for this book is available from the British Library

Library of Congress Cataloging in Publication Data
Farrell, Michael, 1948-
The effective teacher's guide to dyslexia and other learning difficulties
(learning disabilities) : practical strategies / Michael Farrell. – 2nd ed.
p. cm. – (The effective teacher's guides)
Includes bibliographical references and index.
1. Dyslexia – Great Britain. 2. Dyslexic children – Education – Great
Britain. 3. Learning disabled children – Education – Great Britain. I. Title.
LC4710.G7F37 2012
371.91'44 – dc23
2011025224

ISBN: 978-0-415-69384-4 (hbk)
ISBN: 978-0-415-69385-1 (pbk)
ISBN: 978-0-203-15286-7 (ebk)

Typeset in Bembo
by Taylor & Francis Books

MIX
Paper from
responsible sources
FSC
www.fsc.org   FSC® C004839

Printed and bound in Great Britain by
CPI Antony Rowe, Chippenham, Wiltshire

Contents

The Author

Michael Farrell was educated in the United Kingdom. After training as a teacher at Bishop Grosseteste College, Lincoln, and obtaining an Honours degree from Nottingham University, he gained a Masters Degree in Education and Psychology from the Institute of Education, London University. Subsequently, he carried out research for a Master of Philosophy degree at the Institute of Psychiatry, Maudsley Hospital,

London, and for a Doctor of Philosophy degree under the auspices of the Medical Research Council Cognitive Development Unit and London University.

Professionally, Michael Farrell worked as a head teacher, a lecturer at London University and as a local authority inspector. He managed a national psychometric project for City University, London and directed a national initial teacher-training project for the United Kingdom Government Department of Education. His present role as a private special education consultant includes work with children and families, schools, local authorities, voluntary organisations, universities, and government ministries.

His many books, translated into European and Asian languages, include:

- *Foundations of Special Education: An Introduction* (Wiley, 2009).
- *The Special Education Handbook (4th edition)* (David Fulton, 2009).
- *Debating Special Education* (Routledge, 2010).

Preface to Second edition

I am of course extremely pleased to be writing the preface to the second edition of this book, *The Effective Teacher's Guide to Dyslexia and Other Learning Difficulties (Learning Disabilities): Practical strategies*.

It was previously called *The Effective Teacher's Guide to Dyslexia and Other Specific Learning Difficulties: Practical strategies* published in 2006. The first edition attracted favourable comment and I have listened to the views of readers about how the edition might be improved.

I hope it continues to be useful and I again welcome comments from readers to ensure any future editions are as informative and helpful as possible.

Michael Farrell
Herefordshire
dr.m.j.farrell@btopenworld.com

Chapter 1

Introduction

This chapter sets the book in the context of 'The Effective Teacher's Guides' series of which it forms a part. It explains the features of the new edition. I outline the types of disorders with which the book is concerned and then describe the content of subsequent chapters. This introductory chapter then suggests potential readers likely to find the book useful.

'The Effective Teacher's Guides'

'The Effective Teacher's Guides' published by Routledge concern different types of disabilities and disorders. These include cognitive impairment ('learning difficulties' in the United Kingdom and 'mental retardation' in the United States of America), autism, emotional and behavioural disorders, reading disorder and others. Each book in the series describes practical strategies that enable the educational progress and personal and social development of pupils with particular disabilities and disorders.

The other titles are:

- *The Effective Teacher's Guide to Sensory and Physical Impairments: Sensory, Orthopaedic, Motor and Health Impairments, and Traumatic Brain Injury (2nd Edition)*
- *The Effective Teacher's Guide to Behavioural and Emotional Disorders: Disruptive behaviour disorders, anxiety disorders and depressive disorders, and attention deficit hyperactivity disorder (2nd Edition)*
- *The Effective Teacher's Guide to Autism and Communication Difficulties: Practical strategies (2nd Edition)*
- *The Effective Teacher's Guide to Moderate, Severe and Profound Learning Difficulties (Cognitive Impairments): Practical strategies (2nd Edition)*

The new edition

The Effective Teacher's Guide to Dyslexia and Other Learning Difficulties (Learning Disabilities) is the second edition of a book previously published in 2006. It was formerly called *The Effective Teacher's Guide to Dyslexia and Other Specific Learning Difficulties: Practical strategies.*

The first edition was generously reviewed and well received by readers. This new edition seeks to make the content more widely accessible to readers in different countries. The 2006 edition was set within the context of legislation and procedures in the United Kingdom. The new edition focuses more on strategies that work without undue reference to a particular national context. It also includes an extra chapter on 'Disorder of written expression'.

Learning disorders

This section outlines types of disorders with which the book is concerned derived from classifications used in the United States of America and in the United Kingdom.

In the United States of America, pupils considered to need special education covered by federal law have both a defined disability and are considered to need special education because the disability has an adverse educational impact. Categories of disability under federal law as amended in 1997 (20 United States Code 1402, 1997) are reflected in 'designated disability codes' and include the following:

- Specific learning disability (coded 09)

Under 'specific learning disability' is usually included reading disorder, disorder of written expression, and mathematics disorder.

In England, a similar classification (Department for Education and Skills, 2005, passim) comprises:

- Specific learning difficulties

'Specific learning difficulties' are taken to comprise dyslexia, dyscalculia and dyspraxia.

There are different views about the extent to which terms used in different countries or as alternatives in the same country refer to the same condition. Reading disorder is not always taken to mean exactly the same as dyslexia for example. In this book, I tend to use the terms 'reading disorder' to mean broadly the same as 'dyslexia'; and the term 'mathematics disorder' to be similar to 'dyscalculia'. I also include 'developmental co-ordination disorder' and take this to be broadly similar to 'dyspraxia'.

Different views of what constitute learning disabilities

In countries where the term 'specific learning difficulties' is used, there is discussion and some disagreement about what conditions should be included. Kirby and Drew (2003, p. 2) pose the question, 'What conditions fall under the label of specific learning difficulties?' They suggest the conditions include:

- dyslexia
- developmental coordination disorder and
- dyscalculia.

(They discuss whether developmental co-ordination disorder is different to dyspraxia). Kirby and Drew (2003) also include Asperger's syndrome, attention deficit hyperactivity disorder, deficit of motor perception, and dysgraphia. The statement that specific learning disorders 'include' these seven conditions suggests others could be encompassed. Indeed Macintyre and Deponio (2003, pp. 94–99) include 'specific language impairment' (but not dyscalculia). Therefore the conditions that might be considered to be specific learning disorders by others include:

- Asperger's syndrome (a condition with similarities to autism)
- attention deficit hyperactivity disorder (over-activity and difficulty maintaining attention)
- specific language impairment
- dysgraphia (difficulty with writing)
- deficit of attention and motor perception (difficulty involving attention and movement).

One can see that Asperger's syndrome might be considered to have certain similarities to specific learning disorders when compared to autism. That is, Asperger's syndrome can be differentiated from autism by 'lack of cognitive delay' (Ayers and Prytys, 2002, p. 22). But when one considers the breadth of functioning affected by Asperger's syndrome, that is, 'social impairment and restricted patterns of behaviour' (ibid. p. 22) it is also possible to see it as a broader condition. In this series therefore, Asperger's syndrome is considered within the remit of communication and interaction, not as a specific learning disorder.

Similarly, attention deficit hyperactivity disorder might be considered as a specific learning disorder to the extent that it is not associated with cognitive delay. But neither are anxiety disorders, depressive disorders and conduct disorders of themselves associated with cognitive delay and they are not usually considered to be specific learning disorders. In fact there is a case for regarding attention deficit hyperactivity disorder as an emotional and behavioural disorder (as is the case in England) or as a health disorder (as in the United States of America). In this series, I examine attention deficit hyperactivity disorder in the book, *The Effective Teacher's Guide to Behavioural and Emotional Disorders: Disruptive Behaviour Disorders, Anxiety Disorders and Depressive Disorders, and Attention Deficit Hyperactivity Disorder (2nd Edition)*.

Specific language impairment is considered to involve a discrepancy between verbal and non-verbal skills on standardised tests (Macintyre and Deponio, 2003, p. 99). Given that non-verbal skills are relatively unaffected, the condition may be considered 'specific' to language. As one of the books in this series concerns difficulties with communication and interaction (*The Effective Teacher's Guide to Autism and Communication Difficulties*) specific language difficulties are considered there.

Dysgraphia, where there is a difficulty with writing but not a generalised learning difficulty, could be considered a specific learning difficulty. Concerning deficit of attention and motor perception, this is a term used mainly in Scandinavian countries and overlaps with aspects of attention deficit hyperactivity disorder and with aspects of developmental coordination disorder/dyspraxia. Deficit of attention and motor perception are considered in the present text.

How specific are specific learning disabilities?

Learning disabilities are sometimes called 'specific learning difficulties'. The question arises 'How specific are specific learning difficulties'. There are two ways in which this question can be posed. The first concerns the extent to which some conditions do not involve other aspects of cognitive functioning. In considering disabilities of writing, reading and spelling Martin and Miller (2003, p. 59) discuss differentiating 'specific literacy difficulties' from 'general learning difficulties'. With specific literacy difficulties, 'all other functioning is not giving cause for concern'. But these assumptions as they indicate may not be valid (see Stanovich, 1994).

A second way in which one can put the question of the specificity of learning disabilities concerns the co-occurrence of the conditions. A study in Canada (Kaplan *et al.*, 1998) concerned 179 school-aged children assessed for dyslexia, dyspraxia, attention deficit disorder, attention deficit hyperactivity disorder, conduct disorders, depression and anxiety. Fifty per cent of the sample was considered to meet the criteria for two or more of the conditions. In Sweden, a study of the 6–7 year old children in the town of Mariestad identified 10.7 per cent considered to have some kind of neurodevelopmental disorder. All the children with 'deficit of attention and motor perception' had 'developmental co-ordination disorder' and 'attention deficits'. You will notice the conceptual overlap between these. About half met the criteria for attention deficit hyperactivity disorder (Gillberg, 1996).

An aspect of the co-occurrence of some learning disabilities/specific learning difficulties is the overlap of some of the key difficulties associated with some of the conditions. Macintyre and Deponio (2003, p. 7) indicate this in a matrix. They list as 'specific learning difficulties':

- dyspraxia
- dyslexia
- Asperger's syndrome
- specific language impairment
- attention deficit hyperactivity disorder
- attention deficit disorder
- deficit of attention and motor perception.

They then identify fourteen difficulties such as 'literacy' and 'movement fluency' and complete the matrix by showing the existence of many of the difficulties in several of the conditions. Some conditions are associated with a few difficulties while others are linked to many. For example, attention deficit hyperactivity disorder and attention deficit disorder are associated with five of the listed difficulties while dyslexia is linked to twelve and dyspraxia to eleven. The co-occurrence of different conditions looks as though it might be to some extent explained by the overlapping of many of the same difficulties in different conditions. For example, every difficulty is considered to include difficulty with 'social communication'.

At one level, this might suggest that the different conditions are identified according to the series of 'difficulties'. These are common to many of the conditions. Therefore the conditions tend to occur together. In other words, the co-occurrence is simply an artefact of the way the conditions are defined. But there is the possibility that other factors might be important. The various difficulties might suggest elements of common underlying causes of some of the conditions.

Subsequent chapters

Subsequent chapters concern the following topics.

Chapter 2: Reading disorder/dyslexia
Chapter 3: Disorder of written expression/dysgraphia
Chapter 4: Developmental co-ordination disorder/dyspraxia
Chapter 5: Mathematics disorder/dyscalculia
Chapter 6: Summary and conclusion

Each chapter defines and discusses the condition being considered. I then consider provision with regard to: the curriculum and assessment, pedagogy, resources, therapy and care, and school and classroom organisation. The book includes a bibliography and a combined subject and author index.

Proposed readers

I hope readers will include the following:

- teachers and other professionals in mainstream schools, special schools and other settings
- student teachers and teachers in the early years after qualification
- parents
- school managers and administrators
- anyone interested in provision for children and young people with cognitive impairments.

Further reading

Farrell, M. (2009b) (4th. edition) *The Special Education Handbook* London, David Fulton

The book includes entries on various specific learning disorders.

Kauffman, J. M. and Hallahan, D. P. (2005) *Special Education: What It Is and Why We Need It* Boston, MA, Pearson/Allyn and Bacon

This introductory but well-argued book sets out the case for special education and explains some of its main features.

Reynolds, C. R. and Fletcher-Janzen, E. (Eds.) (2004) (2nd. Edition) *Concise Encyclopaedia of Special Education: A Reference for the Education of Handicapped and Other Exceptional Children and Adults* Hoboken, NY, John Wiley and Sons

This reference work includes reviews of assessment instruments, biographies, teaching approaches, and overviews of disabilities and disorders.

Chapter 2

Reading disorder/dyslexia

Introduction

This chapter looks at definitions of reading disorder; its prevalence; some characteristics of reading difficulties; causal factors; and identification and assessment. It considers possible associated difficulties, their assessment and related provision. I look at provision for reading and for reading skills, reading fluency and reading comprehension. The chapter examines alternative and augmentative communication. The final section summarises provision in relation to curriculum and assessment; pedagogy; resources; therapy/care; and school and classroom organisation.

Definitions

The *Diagnostic and Statistical Manual of Mental Disorders Fourth Edition Text Revision* (DSM-IV-TR) (American Psychiatric Association, 2000, pp. 51–53) defines reading disorder. Reading achievement is 'substantially below' what is expected given the child's age, measured intelligence and education. Reading achievement is assessed in terms of reading accuracy, speed, or comprehension measured by individually administered standardised tests. Reading disorder 'significantly' hinders academic achievement of daily living activities requiring reading skills. Oral reading is characterised by 'distortions, substitutions or omissions' (ibid. p.52). Oral and silent reading both tend to be slow and involve comprehension errors. Developmental delays in language may occur in association with reading disorder (and other learning disabilities).

The judgement that reading achievement is 'substantially below' expectations is often taken to mean two or more standard deviations below the expected level. In special circumstances, one standard deviation may be considered sufficient, for example where the disorder has had a significant impact on performance in the test of general intelligence (Fonagy *et al.*, 2005, p. 360).

Contrary to the implications of the criteria of the American Psychiatric Association (2000, pp. 51–53), there is growing consensus that reading disorder has to be associated with reading achievement below age expectations. Previously, some observers supported an achievement intelligence quotient (IQ) discrepancy view. This viewed reading impairment in terms of a discrepancy between a child's actual reading score and the reading score that would be predicted on the basis of chronological age or IQ (or both).

Discrepancy scores are defined as the difference between the score on a specified reading test and the score predicted from the regression of reading performance on a measure of IQ (that is the correlation between reading and IQ). A discrepancy of a specified value is taken as a measure of underachievement in reading. In the IQ-achievement discrepancy view, a child could be considered to have reading disorder if he performed at age average or better in reading achievement but had a high IQ suggesting he should be doing even better. Accordingly, Miles and Miles (1990, p. iv) could claim, 'there is no contradiction in saying that a person is dyslexic while never the less being a competent reader'.

Typical of the modern view is that of Beitchman and Young (1997) who reviewed studies over the previous ten years. They recommend that if a child is not functioning below the expected level for age or grade, he is unlikely to require special help. He should not be considered to have a learning disorder even though there may be a substantial IQ-achievement discrepancy. Similarly, Dykman and Ackerman (1992) comment on provision for dyslexia in the public school system (the public school system in the United States of America parallels the maintained school system in the United Kingdom). They observe,

'Regression formulas are well and good if the purpose is to identify all students who are underachievers. But it defies common sense to diagnose a child with an IQ of 130 and a reading standard score of 110 as having dyslexia. Certainly the public school system should not be expected to offer special services to such a child.'

There are differences between some definitions of 'reading disorder' and 'dyslexia'. Some definitions of dyslexia include disorder of written expression. The American Psychiatric Association (2000) criteria separate reading disorder and disorder of written expression while acknowledging the two often occur together. Mathematics disorder is also commonly associated with reading disorder.

Where research refers to dyslexia, it sometimes defines this in terms of a discrepancy view. When consulting research you need to be careful to identify the position of the researchers on these questions of definition. Different types of dyslexia have been suggested such as 'visual dyslexia' and 'verbal dyslexia'.

Prevalence

The prevalence of reading disorder is not easy to ascertain. Many studies fail to separate out disorders of reading, written expression and mathematics. In different countries, prevalence rates vary according to the strictness of criteria. In the United States of America it is estimated that about 4 per cent of school aged children experience reading disorder.

More boys than girls are usually considered to have reading disorder. However, it appears that referral of boys may be increased because of associated behaviour difficulties. When careful diagnostic procedures are used (rather than school referral) a more equal gender balance is found (American Psychiatric Association, 2000, p. 52).

Causal factors

In exclusionary definitions, dyslexia is in part defined by excluding causation by general intellectual impairment, socio cultural constraints or emotional factors. Among factors associated with reading disorder are:

- phonological difficulties
- visual difficulties and visual processing difficulties
- auditory perception and auditory processing difficulties
- short-term verbal memory difficulties; and sequencing difficulties (temporal order).

Each of these can be seen as explaining something about literacy problems. If a child has phonological difficulties the relationship between the sound related aspects of language and the written text are likely to be problematic. Such associated factors can be said to contribute to reading disorder although the relationship may be reciprocal.

One might also reflect on how the 'associated difficulties' might have arisen. What led to the problems with information processing? Sometimes in connection with such issues, biological explanations are offered.

Studies considering heritable factors have implicated loci on chromosomes 2, 3, 6, 15, and 18 (Fisher and DeFries, 2002) for the transmission of phonological awareness deficits and subsequent difficulties with reading. The detailed consequences of these findings are still to be developed.

Research involving functional brain imaging with children and adults with dyslexia indicates a failure of left hemisphere posterior brain systems to function correctly during reading (Paulesu *et al.*, 2001). The area of the brain known as the planum temporale is normally asymmetrical with the left side being greater than the right. But in some individuals with developmental dyslexia it has been found to be more symmetrical (Hynd *et al.*, 1990).

Identification and assessment

The teacher or the child's parents may have concerns about perceived slow progress or difficulties with reading. You may gather evidence to consider further and consult with others such as senior teaching colleagues or school psychologists. A speech pathologist may be consulted, for example, where you think the child may have phonological difficulties.

Certain characteristics are associated with reading difficulties. The child may when reading:

- hesitate over words;
- confuse letters with similar shapes such as 'u' and 'n', visually similar words like 'was' and 'saw' and small words such as 'it' and 'is';
- omit small words such as 'it' and 'is', other words, or word endings; or
- make errors regarding semantically related words (reading 'cat' for 'dog'), polysyllabic words ('animal', 'corridor', 'family' and so on), or grammar (including inconsistent use of tense).

Therefore the identification and assessment of difficulties with reading is likely to include:

- a profile of the sorts of errors that the pupil makes (relating to the characteristics outlined above), for example using miscue analysis;
- an indication of how the pupil reads (e.g. whether he is hesitant over words);
- an indication of whether the pupil tends to prefer silent reading or reading aloud and whether one leads to better comprehension than the other.

Commercial assessments of 'dyslexia' are available in developed countries, standardised for the country concerned. They sample component skills or necessary skills relating to reading such as rapid naming, phonemic segmentation, verbal fluency, backwards digit span, assessment of syllable and phoneme deletions (aimed at identifying phonological processing ability) and so on. Assessment implications of associated difficulties are touched on in the next section.

Possible associated difficulties, their assessment and related provision

It is important that various sub skills relating to reading work together. If one or more sub skills are dysfunctional, the pupil may find it hard to improve the skill while simultaneously maintaining other component skills of reading. In reading the pupil has to:

- visually focus on words effectively and track words across a written page;
- auditorily discriminate, sequence, blend and segment sounds in words;
- retain information in short term memory while it is processed; and
- organise information.

Where these are underpinning skills or necessary skills, the pupil may find it difficult to improve them while sustaining other skills. Therefore it is assumed it is beneficial to approach some skills distinctively. A learner's other skills may also be used to compensate for weakness. Consider a pupil having difficulties with auditory processing and with blending and segmenting sounds in words. This may be compensated for by multi-sensory methods, including teaching phonics linking visual and kinaesthetic modes with word sounds.

Phonological difficulties

Phonology difficulties involve problems relating speech sounds to changes in meaning. Phonological knowledge enables the speaker to understand that, when a speech sound is changed into a word, meaning changes. Speakers normally come to learn distinctions such as 'dog'/'log' or 'pig'/'pin'. Hearing his own speech, the speaker modifies it as necessary to make the required word. The phonological system lays down a sort of phonological representation of the speech sound sequence at a cognitive level of language functioning. This helps the process to be automatic. Speakers draw on this phonological representation when developing awareness of the different sounds in a word. In reading English, the forty-four speech sounds are linked to written marks or graphemes, enabling the child to develop a phoneme–grapheme correspondence.

The phonological deficit theory maintains that in reading disorder, the main cognitive deficit is in the ability to represent or recall phonemes:

a problem with phonological representations. This phonological deficit leads to the poor mental mapping of letters of the alphabet to phonemes. Both the phonological deficit and the poor letter–phoneme mapping operate at the cognitive level. Behaviourally, both lead to difficulties with phonological tasks such as splitting words into their phonemes. Also, poor letter–phoneme mapping relates to reading difficulties.

There is extensive evidence in support of a phonological deficit theory. People with reading disorder have difficulty retaining speech in short term memory and consciously breaking it up into phonemes. A person with reading disorder will tend to have difficulty deleting or substituting phonemes from words (Snowling, 2000). A phonological deficit in children at the age of 6 years was found in a Norwegian study to be a strong predictor of reading difficulties (Hagtvet, 1997). Speech rate has been identified as a predictor of dyslexic difficulties (Hulme and Snowling, 1997). A double deficit of phonological processing and naming speed has been suggested (Wolf and O'Brien, 2001)

In an alphabetical system the brain has to map the letters of the alphabet onto a mental representation of corresponding phonemes. Problems representing and recalling phonemes is expected to lead to reading difficulties. However, the exact nature of the phonological deficit and its biological concomitants is not fully understood.

Identifying and assessing phonological difficulties is likely to include assessing expressive language. You assess whether it includes errors, omissions or other difficulties in conversation or classroom interaction. These may suggest difficulties relating to the key meaningful elements of sound. You will also be likely to assess whether the child has difficulty with the comprehension of speech. For example the child may appear not to understand instructions or questions. This could indicate difficulty with the elements of speech conveying meaning.

Information from assessment can suggest strategies to help the child's learning or identify strategies the child has already developed. Assessment could indicate that mode of 'input' (verbal, written or visual) appears to aid comprehension. This could indicate a preference for visual input that might help comprehension where there are phonological difficulties. Or the child's expressive language can be observed in different contexts to see if communication is easier in some.

Where there are serious phonological difficulties, you may work with a speech pathologist to develop and oversee suitable programmes. The learner may be taught to become more aware of and to use in spoken language, sounds and sequences of sounds that convey meaning in speech. In his own speech, the pupil may practise sounds he frequently misses, such as those at the beginnings and endings of words.

Similarly, speech comprehension practice is used to help the pupil notice key sounds that convey meaning and changes in meaning. The student can be taught to listen for and recognise the sound 's' at the end of a word when it signals a plural as in 'cat' and 'cats'. Speech comprehension can be aided by other sensory modes. You can show accompanying pictures or objects such as a picture of one 'cat' and several 'cats'. Take care to establish that the difficulty is predominantly phonological rather than mainly grammatical.

To raise phonological awareness, where new vocabulary is introduced, you can encourage pupils' interest in a word or phrase. Explicitly teach and check the pupils' understanding of various aspects of the vocabulary: semantic and grammatical as well as phonological. Phonological aspects may include asking questions.

'How do the sounds of the word break up and blend back together?'
'Do you know any similar sounding words?'
'What are syllables of the word?' (Younger children may enjoy clapping these out).

This can be routinely and briefly accomplished when key words are introduced at the beginning of a lesson, in both elementary/primary schools and high/secondary schools where subject specialists can use the method to reinforce new vocabulary.

An approach drawing on interest in speech sounds is Metaphon, designed to bring about phonological change through enhancing knowledge of the phonological and communicative aspects of language (Howell and Dean, 1994, p. vii). The *Metaphon Resource Pack* (Dean *et al.*, 1990) is used with children aged 3 years 6 months to 7 years. It provides phonological assessment giving information about the child's pronunciation abilities.

Visual processing difficulties

Visual factors concern:

- convergence
- accommodation
- tracking.

Convergence involves the eyes converging on letters of print or handwriting at a distance of about 30 centimetres to ensure that the brain receives a unified picture of the letters and words. For some children with dyslexia, there may be visual convergence difficulties that may lead to binocular instability (Stein, 1995).

Accommodation involves being able to quickly adjust eye focus to changing circumstances. This includes changing distances between page and eye as the eye moves down a page of writing. Difficulties with this clearly affect reading, writing and spelling.

Tracking involves the skill of scanning a line of print from word to word and line to line while keeping one's place. Difficulties with this lead to losing one's place in reading. More likely 'abnormal eye movements are a consequence rather than a cause of reading disability' (Beaton, 2004, p. 219).

Some people with dyslexia appear to have difficulties with visual tasks such as those involving the perception of movement. One attempt to explain such findings is the magnocellular theory. This is based on a distinction between two proposed neuronal pathways of the visual system: the magnocellular and parvocellular. It is hypothesised that the magnocellular system is abnormal in people with reading disorder. This causes difficulties in some aspects of visual perception and in binocular control that may lead to a reading difficulty. Impaired development of the magnocellular component of the visual system, which processes fast temporal information, may lead to visual confusions. Letters may look blurred or appear to move round (Stein *et al.*, 2001).

At the neurological level then there is considered to be a general magnocellular dysfunction. This leads to a visual magnocellular deficit and a temporal auditory deficit at the cognitive level (the temporal auditory deficit is believed to lead to the phonological deficit). Behaviourally, the visual magnocellular deficit is hypothesised to lead to difficulties with certain visual tasks, such as those requiring the perception of motion, and to reading difficulties. The temporal auditory deficit is thought to lead to, behaviourally, difficulties with certain auditory tasks requiring the perception of brief or rapid speech (or non speech) sounds.

The assessment of visual difficulties is likely to involve two features. The first is that the student has age inappropriate difficulty discriminating between letters that appear the same ('m' and 'n') or that are the same but in different forms ('M' and 'm'). The second feature is that the learner omits or transposes part of a word (which could indicate a difficulty with visual segmentation).

Turning to interventions, where visual discrimination is poor the teacher may use one or more books or activities aimed at encouraging this skill. These may include several pictures of objects including one that is obviously different and progress to series where the difference is increasingly subtle. You may use a series of letters with one letter that is obviously different, progressing to series where the difference is subtler.

Practice in discriminating letters can involve over-learning one letter, for example, 'm'. You then introduce a letter with which the child often confuses it such as 'n'. Pupils may be directly taught the upper and lower case forms of the same letter. To aid segmentation, items may be used first. Using a row of coloured bricks, you ask the pupil to space them into sets of one, or two, or three. Printed letters of the alphabet can later be used to form words and the pupil asked to make segments such as 'b' 'at' or 'su' 'n'.

Practice in tracking can involve exercises requiring the pupil to give close attention to the text and track it from left to right (in English). For example, the learner can be encouraged to track along a sentence or sentences marking first the letter 'a' then the letter 'b' then 'c' and so on (e.g. The **a**pple was **b**ig and **c**old and ...).

'Scotopic sensitivity' is particular sensitivity to print on black paper. Irlen (1994) found that some students in high school and at university who were poor readers had a particular sensitivity to black print on white paper. This was especially so where the print was faint, the paper was glossy and fluorescent lighting was used. Words appeared to move around the page and the glare from the page tended to cause eye irritation. For some learners, spectacles with tinted lenses or coloured page overlays appear to reduce the glare and stabilise the image of words on the page.

Auditory perception and auditory processing difficulties

Auditory perception and auditory processing difficulties are relevant. This is because some perceptual aspects of speech are relevant to developing phonemic awareness, so reading ability may be related to speech perception. One aspect of auditory perception concerns phonetic categorisation. In making different speech sounds, there are different durations between the instant that air is released from the lips and the vocal cords vibrating (voice onset time). This is important as a cue in speech perception. Presenting sounds using a speech synthesiser, with a 0 millisecond (msec.) voice-onset time, produces a perception of a /ba/ sound. A 40 msec. voice onset time leads to a perception of a /pa/ sound. At voice onset times between 0 and 40 msec. people report hearing either a /ba/ or a /pa/ sound, not a sound somewhere between, a phenomenon known as categorical perception.

Some children with dyslexia have been found to be less consistent in their classification of stimuli and changed more gradually from one phonetic category to another than did a control group of children (Godfrey et al., 1981, p. 419–20). It was suggested that this inconsistency in phonetic categorisation might impair the ability to learn through forming 'inadequate long term representations of phonetic units'. This could adversely affect the reading process of transforming script into phonetic units of speech and ordering and combining those units that constitute words.

The assessment of auditory processing difficulties is likely to involve identifying:

- difficulties with auditory discrimination
- difficulties with auditory sequencing, blending and segmentation and
- inability to perceive consonant sounds in different positions.

Auditory discrimination may be practised by encouraging the pupil to make progressively finer distinctions in set tasks and exercises. An example is recognising and discriminating sounds, including letter sounds from an audio recording.

Auditory segmenting and blending can be taught and practised. For example you can play an audio recording and ask the pupil to listen for certain sounds (such as 'to'). The sounds would be obvious and the pace slow at first ('I am going out **to**morrow')

Auditory blending can be taught using phonics approaches such as those in Phonographix™ (www.readamerica.net) which introduces letter sounds and then their blends in teaching reading.

Multi-sensory teaching and learning may help auditory processing weakness. This is because other preferred modes are likely to be presented. These may reinforce learning in the weaker (auditory) mode, for example by supplementing the spoken word by visual aids and gesture.

The pupil can be taught to listen to consonant sounds in different positions, for example by listening for the final consonant in the words, 'dog', 'log' and 'doll' or the initial consonant in 'pit', 'pot' and 'dot' and identifying the odd one out.

Short-term verbal memory difficulties

Studies of dyslexia have found problems with verbal memory and learning, especially in tasks requiring phonological processes (Share, 1995). Children with dyslexia tend to have lower digit spans than control readers (McDougal et al., 1994). One possible explanation is that difficulties with verbal memory in some children with dyslexia relate to difficulties in phonological awareness. This is because memory difficulties make it harder to keep in mind individual phonemes as part of a phonic reading strategy (Beaton, 2004, p. 72). Other research suggests that good readers are more likely to use verbal retrieval strategies or rehearsal strategies than poor readers (Palmer, 2000).

Memory span is longer for words than for pseudo words of the same length. This suggests that when remembering lists of items, it is easier to remember words from established representations in long-term memory. It is thought (Hulme and Snowling, 1997) that a partially decayed memory trace may be reconstructed from stored knowledge about the structure of words. For learners with dyslexia, this knowledge may be inefficiently represented. If so, it would offer only limited help in supporting the process of reconstruction, resulting in lower recall performance for learners with dyslexia. Identifying and assessing memory difficulties may include identifying a profile of the areas and circumstances in which these difficulties are apparent.

Short-term memory difficulties can be aided by encouraging the pupil to be aware of the settings and conditions he finds conducive to memorising well. These might include actively focusing on the task in hand. The student would not try to do something else at the same time and would avoid distractions by using a quiet place. Your requests and instructions to students are more likely to be processed and remembered if given one at a time.

Embedding in memory (using long term memory) is facilitated if the pupil is interested and can relate the new information and ideas to what he already knows. This suggests teachers find out the pupil's interests and encourage him to relate new information to these. Multi-sensory methods may be used and the material to be remembered should be well organised. Recall and recognition can be aided by drawing on different sensory modes and particular ways that are used in presenting, recording and studying the information. These include diagrams or mnemonics.

Sequencing difficulties (temporal order)

Several studies have found poor readers less able to remember the serial order of events than average or good readers. In one study, participants were required to reproduce a sequence of taps on a wooden block or to repeat a sequence of digits. A relationship was found between the accuracy of recall of sequence of events and reading attainment (Corkin, 1974). A temporal processing deficit has been proposed. It possibly involves a 'high degree of processing overlap associated with the parallel transmission of speech' (Share, 1995, p. 188). This could lead to poor phonological representations.

Such a deficit could explain difficulties in the fast sequencing of speech motor acts needed for 'serial naming and verbal rehearsal' (p.188). Identifying sequencing difficulties is likely to focus on information such as sequencing letters of the alphabet, words when reading.

Using various senses can assist learning sequences such as letters of the alphabet. The pupil places pieces of card each bearing a letter in front of him in an arc with the 'a' on the left and the 'z' on the right. Learning the letters in blocks reinforcing rhythm may help:

- 'a' through 'g'
- 'h' through 'n'
- 'o' through 'u'
- 'v' through 'z'.

Handling and laying out the cards uses kinaesthetic memory. Speaking the letter sounds and hearing others saying them uses auditory memory. Seeing the letters employs visual memory. These three all help to establish the sequence (Pollock *et al.*, 2004, pp. 118–19). This has implications where a dictionary, encyclopaedia or other alphabetically organised reference book is used. The pages can be marked by tabs to separate the alphabetical sequence in the same way that the blocks of letters were learned, divided at 'g', 'n' and 'u'. This makes the required word easier to find.

Provision for reading skills

Early intervention: direct code instruction

Foorman and colleagues (1998) assessed the reading development of 285 children in first and second grade in 66 classrooms in several Title 1 schools in Texas. The children had scored in the lowest 18 per cent on an early literacy assessment used by the school district. Three programmes were compared with the standard curriculum for the district. The three programmes provided interventions as follows:

1   direct instruction in letter-sound correspondences and practice decoding text (direct code)
2   less direct instruction in letter-sound correspondences embedded in authentic literature samples (embedded code)
3   implicit instruction in the alphabetic code while children read authentic text (implicit code).

Children in the direct code approach showed better word identification skills and steeper learning curves in word reading than did children experiencing the implicit code instruction. This was especially so for children entering with the lowest levels of phonological awareness. Population based failure rates derived from this study suggested that 6 per cent of children would remain relatively weak in reading development (Torgesen, 2000). This suggests a remaining issue of how to improve the reading development of the most severe forms of reading disability.

Phonological training

Brooks (2002) reviewed and evaluated the effectiveness of various schemes in the report, *What Works for Reading Difficulties?* Among the interventions examined was Phonographix[TM]. This approach takes as important the fact that English orthography is an alphabet for representing originally and in principle each distinctive speech sound with one symbol. Phonographix [TM] (www.readamerica.net) develops the notion that written English is a phonemic code with each sound in a spoken word being represented by some part of the written version. It teaches the phonological skills of blending, segmenting and phoneme manipulation required to use a phonemic code, explicitly teaching correspondences in sound-to-symbol relationships. It provided the largest ratio gain of all the studies reviewed in the Brooks report.

'Reading Intervention' was also reviewed and evaluated in the report, *What Works for Reading Difficulties?* (Brooks, 2002) It combines phonological training with reading. This enables pupils to isolate phonemes in words. Students can come to recognise that sounds can be common between words and that specific sounds can be represented by certain letters. In one study poor readers aged 6 to 7 years were randomly assigned to one of four groups:

1 received systematic training in phonological skills to promote phonological awareness and help in learning to read
2 received training in reading only
3 received training only in phonological skills
4 received normal teaching (controls)

Experimental groups 1, 2 and 3 received 40 sessions of 30 minutes each over a period of 20 weeks. In group 1 the sessions were in three parts. The first part involved the child reading a familiar book with the teacher making a written record so the child could go over familiar words in different contexts. This also involved phonological activities and letter identification using a multi-sensory approach of feeling, writing and naming. The second part of the session involved writing a story and cutting it up. The third part introduced a new book.

The reading plus phonology group (group 1) made significantly better progress than other groups (Hatcher, 2000). Brooks states the initiative continues to be effective for poor readers, 'and even for children with moderate learning difficulties or dyslexia' (Brooks, 2002, p. 39). Some studies supporting this intervention take a discrepancy view of dyslexia and readers may wish to consider the original reports carefully when judging applicability.

Combination programmes

An intervention study by Olsen, Wise and colleagues (Wise, Ring and Olsen, 2000) combined:

(a) features of an oral-motor programme for training phonological awareness, reading, and spelling skills (The Lindamood Auditory Discrimination in Depth programme);
(b) the researchers' own computer-based reading training programme called Reading with Orthographic and Speech Support.

Two groups of children with reading disabilities from grades 2 through 5 received phonological decoding and digitised speech to help them read unknown words in story reading on the computer. With this training one group received further phonological awareness training using the Auditory Discrimination in Depth programme oral-motor methods. The second group received extra training in reading comprehension strategies.

The first group (receiving extra phonological awareness training) was better than the second group at phonological awareness and phonological decoding skill. This was so immediately after training and a year later. But they were not superior in word recognition performance at one and two year follow up assessments. It appears there is a problem with generalising the improved phonological skills to word recognition.

Assisting the generalisation of phonological skills to reading

Research was carried out at the Hospital for Sick Children in Toronto, Canada with children with severe reading disabilities. It included reading interventions aimed at the problem of generalising instructional gains in word identification learning.

One approach was the Phonological Analysis and Blending/Direct Instruction programme. It comprises programmes training phonological analysis, phonological blending, and letter-sound association skills. This is done in the context of intensive and systematic word recognition and decoding instruction.

Another approach was Word Identification Strategy Training. This instructs the child through teacher led dialogue, and teaches how to use and monitor the application of four metacognitive decoding strategies. Its word identification strategies include 'peeling off' suffixes and prefixes in a multisyllabic word, and identifying parts of a word you already know. It includes a metacognitive 'game plan' to train flexibility in choice of strategy and the evaluation of their success.

Both of these approaches helped pupils generalise remedial gains. Positive effects were found even with children with the most severe reading disabilities (Lovett, Stienbach and Frijters, 2000).

Another study (Lovett et al., 2000) involved eighty-five children aged 7–13 years and having severe reading disability. They were randomly assigned to seventy hours of remedial instruction in one of five conditions:

- Phonological Analysis and Blending/Direct Instruction programme followed by Word Identification Strategy Training
- Word Identification Strategy Training followed by Phonological Analysis and Blending/Direct Instruction programme
- Phonological Analysis and Blending/Direct Instruction programme repeated
- Word Identification Strategy Training repeated
- Classroom Survival Skills (study skills) followed by mathematics.

Each child's skills were assessed before (once), during the programme (three times) and afterwards (once). This was done using standard measures of word recognition, passage comprehension, and non-word reading. The most superior outcomes and steepest learning curves were found for children in the group that had experienced Phonological Analysis and Blending/Direct Instruction programme followed by Word Identification Strategy Training. This condition was superior to each method alone on:

- measures of phonological reading skill (non word reading)
- tests of letter sound and key word knowledge
- three word identification measures.

Generalisation from non-word decoding to other reading measures it appears can be best achieved through a combination of remedial components. Also, a review of intervention studies indicated that optimal approaches in instructing children with learning disabilities combine direct instruction and strategy instruction methods (Swanson and Hoskyn, 1998).

A programme, the PHAST Track Reading Programme (Phonological and Strategy Training) for 'struggling readers' seeks to integrate the two approaches into a single programme (Lovett et al., 2000). It has been extended to include reading comprehension, writing and spelling lessons. An adaptation PHAST PACES was developed for older (high school) readers and young adults.

Reading fluency

RAVE-O (Retrieval, Automaticity, Vocabulary elaboration, Engagement with language, Orthography) is an experimental reading programme intended to aid the development of reading fluency (Wolf, Miller and Donnelly, 2000). It is taught in combination with a systematic phonologically based programme teaching letter-sound knowledge, decoding, and word identification skills while remediating speech based phonological processes. In combination with this, RAVE-O aims to:

- develop accuracy and automaticity in reading sub skills and component processes;
- aid the development of fluency in word identification, word attack, and text reading, and comprehension processes;
- change the attitudes and feelings of pupils with reading disability in their approach to words and written language.

RAVE-O encourages children to learn to play with language through animated computer games, building imaginative word webs, instruction in word retrieval strategies that are playful but systematic, and reading one-minute mystery stories.

Provision for reading comprehension

Reading comprehension involves getting the gist or 'main idea' from a text. Once a learner has the main idea, he can draw inferences from the text. Difficulty with reading comprehension may be the result of lack of fluency in word recognition. It may also be related to cognitive processing problems. These include limitations in working memory, lexical processing difficulties, poor inference making and poor monitoring of comprehension (Gersten *et al.*, 2001).

Work has been carried out on helping pupils grasp the main idea of texts. Normally achieving children in the fourth to sixth grades were given a reading comprehension task. They were asked to read a short paragraph and select an appropriate title from several choices and write a summary sentence for the paragraph. Performance was better when pupils had to only select the main idea from an array than when they had to formulate a summary sentence. This was replicated with children with learning disabilities (Taylor and Williams, 1983).

However, pupils with learning disabilities differed from younger children without learning disabilities in their response to the inclusion of information that was unrelated to the main idea of the paragraph. Children without learning disabilities were able to identify the anomalous sentence the closer it was to the end of the paragraph but children with learning disabilities were not. This suggested that pupils with learning disabilities were less able to gradually build up a representation as the information in each successive sentence was processed.

From this work, an instructional sequence was developed. It used simple, highly structured paragraphs. It also emphasised a clear definition of what a 'main idea' is and a clear description of the task. In evaluating the model, 11-year-old children with learning disabilities were found after 10 lessons to be better at identifying anomalous sentences and writing sentences on the materials (Williams *et al.*, 1983).

In a similar way, research has been conducted into how pupils understand the theme of a story. An instructional model for pupils with learning disabilities was developed from this. The instruction involved teacher explanation and modelling, guided practice, and independent practice. (For summaries of this and related work, see Williams, 2003, pp. 293–305).

Alternative and augmentative communication

Symbolic communication uses symbols such as a word or picture to stand for something. 'Non aided' communication involves the child making a movement or vocalisation that does not necessitate a physical aid or other device (Vanderheiden and Lloyd, 1986). 'Aided' augmentative communication involves using a device or item such as a communication board, eye gaze board or electronic system. Three categories have been suggested (Bigge, Best and Wolff Heller, 2001, p. 237).

Non-electronic devices may include communication boards and communication notebooks. Communication books can include photographs, symbols and words. These enable a pupil to find a symbol and show the particular page to someone who may not know the symbol so they can see the intended word.

Dedicated communication devices are electronic communication systems that speak programmed messages when the user activates locations marked by symbols. Computer based communication systems may consist of a computer with input options, communication software, and a speech synthesizer.

Computer aided communication may involve the pupil having a voice production device with a computer based bank of words and sentences that can be produced by pressing the keyboard keys.

Symbols may be part or whole objects used to represent an item or activity. In a symbol system using graphical communication, each symbol represents a concept such as an object, person, activity or attribute. With communication grids several symbols are set out in a specified order. Such grids can enable a pupil to participate in group sessions; for example, to support the retelling of a story. A sequence of symbols can be used to indicate a sequence of activities, including a school timetable for a pupil. Computer technology, using symbols, allows a large number of symbols to be used flexibly. There are symbol e-mail programmes, and websites that use symbols.

Curriculum and assessment; pedagogy; resources; therapy/care; and organisation

Curriculum

Given the centrality of reading to most subjects of the curriculum, the levels of curriculum for pupils with reading disorder are likely to be lower than those for other children. The curriculum will recognise this so that the pupil's progress can move from secure foundations. The balance of subjects may emphasise language and reading with necessary support. Within subjects the reading element will be an important focus of support.

Small steps of assessment may be used with regard to language and reading to ensure progress is recognised. The curriculum may include programmes such as some of those described earlier in the chapter that combine curriculum content, approaches to pedagogy and specific resources.

Pedagogy

Teaching and learning approaches may include support for any evident visual and visual processing difficulties. Approaches might ensure materials avoid difficult tracking from one plane to another where possible. Pedagogy will also focus on phonological development; auditory perception training; support for difficulties with short-term memory; and help with sequencing difficulties. Strategies are used to facilitate reading fluency and comprehension.

Resources

Computer software that supports reading is also used. Materials such as printed lessons and computer activities associated with particular programmes may be used. Where symbols are used, the relevant resources are of course necessary. For a few pupils with visual processing difficulties, tinted lenses may be considered.

Therapy/care

The speech and language pathologist may work directly or in a consultancy role to help with phonological difficulties.

Organisation

There do not appear to be any distinctive aspects of school and classroom organisation that are essential for reading disorder.

Thinking points

Readers may wish to consider:

- how convincing they find the view that, if reading disorder is associated with underlying difficulties, working directly on these will improve reading;
- the extent to which direct approaches to improving reading appear to tackle supposed related difficulties.

Key texts

Beaton, A. A. (2004) *Dyslexia, Reading and the Brain: A Sourcebook of Biological and Psychological Research* London, Psychology Press

A lucid and balanced presentation of a vast amount of research relating to reading and reading difficulties.

Klingner, J., Vaughn, S. and Boardman A. (2007) *Teaching Reading Comprehension to Students with Learning Difficulties* New York, Guilford Press

Research based recommendations for the classroom.

Rosen, G. D. (2006) *The Dyslexic Brain: New Pathways in Neuroscience Discovery* New York, Taylor and Francis

Examines neural components and functions involved in reading, possible sources of breakdown and interventions.

Swanson, H. L., Harris, K. R. and Graham, S. (Eds.) (2003) *Handbook of Learning Disabilities* New York, Guilford Press

A well structured overview of learning difficulties covering: foundations and current perspectives; causes and behavioural manifestations; effective instruction; formation of instructional models; and methodology.

Chapter 3

Disorder of written expression/ dysgraphia

Introduction

This chapter looks at a definition of disorder of written expression, prevalence, causal factors, identification and assessment, and traditional and process based approaches to teaching writing. In provision for writing and spelling, I examine: remediating sequencing, improving co-ordination skills for handwriting, and teaching cursive script.

Turning to provision for writing composition, the chapter looks at frameworks for writing, reducing task demands, software for essay structure, note taking, writing for a purpose, and developing self regulation strategies. For spelling, it considers: multi-sensory aspects, Directed Spelling Thinking Activity, and target words.

Although the chapter is concerned mainly with traditional orthography, it next considers the important matter of alternative and augmentative communication including the use of symbols. In the final section, I summarise provision in terms of curriculum and assessment; pedagogy; resources; therapy/care; and organisation.

Definition

It is recognised that there are 'complex skills and sub-skills' involved in writing. Some of these are organising ideas, forming letters, spelling and punctuation (Macintyre and Deponio, 2003, p. 67). The necessary abilities range from those associated with 'lower level transcription skills' to ones needed for 'higher level composing' (Gregg and Mather, 2002, p. 7). The interrelationships of reading and writing are also recognised (Nelson and Calfee, 1998, passim).

The *Diagnostic and Statistical Manual of Mental Disorders Fourth Edition Text Revision* (DSM-IV-TR) (American Psychiatric Association, 2000, pp. 54–56) outlines what it sees as the essential features of disorder of written expression. Individually administered standardised tests of writing skills or functional assessment are used. These assessments indicate that writing skills are substantially below age expectations, measured intelligence and 'age appropriate education'. Being substantially below age expectations is often taken to mean two standard deviations below average. The disorder hinders academic achievement or daily living activities requiring the composition of written texts.

There is generally a combination of difficulties. These are indicated by errors in grammar and punctuation in written sentences, poor organisation of paragraphs, many spelling errors, and very poor handwriting. Disorder in spelling and handwriting alone is not considered to meet the definition of disorder of written expression. Poor handwriting may be the result of impaired motor co-ordination. Where this is the case, it is suggested that a 'diagnosis' of developmental co-ordination disorder be considered (American Psychiatric Association, 2000, p. 56).

Both disorder of written expression and mathematics disorder are commonly associated with reading disorder. It is comparatively rare for either mathematics disorder or disorder of written expression to be found in the absence of reading disorder (American Psychiatric Association, 2000, p. 52). Language deficits and perceptual motor deficits may accompany disorder of written expression (ibid. p. 55).

Prevalence

Prevalence is difficult to establish because disorder of written expression is not often differentiated from reading disorder or mathematics disorder in research studies. However, developmental disorder of written expression appears to occur in about 4 per cent of children. Boys are three times more likely to meet the criteria (Kavale and Forness, 1995).

Causal factors

The skills of spelling and handwriting influence the development of competency in written expression. Even leaving these aside there are still the components of executive functions (Wong, 1991) and semantic knowledge (Berninger, 1994) that are required. The complexity of the processes has perhaps been a factor in constraining research in this area. As Westwood (2003) points out, 'Competence in writing relies heavily on competence in listening, speaking and reading, as well as on possession of necessary strategies for planning, encoding, reviewing and revising written language' (p. 51). Pupils with learning difficulties tend to have great difficulties with writing particularly with planning, sequencing ideas, editing and revising (Hess and Wheldall, 1999).

Sandler and colleagues (1992) suggested possible subtypes of 'written language disorder' drawing on cluster analysis of data. The first group, which was also the largest, had fine motor and linguistic deficits. The second had poor handwriting and visual spatial skills but good spelling and good ability to develop ideas. The third group had memory and attention problems. The fourth had difficulties with letter production, legibility and sequencing.

Many areas of the brain appear to be implicated in the complex activity of written expression. A central factor in disorder of written expression may be executive and working memory deficits. These have been associated with such aspects as poor sentence coherence and lexical cohesion (Wilson and Proctor, 2000).

Assessment

While there are many standardised assessments of spelling ability, fewer such tests exist for writing. The teacher and others will need to compare several examples of the child's writing with that of other children developing age typically. You may need to consult others and also take into account the child's intellectual ability. Examples of the child's writing may be compared that involve copying, writing from dictation, and writing spontaneously. It is not usually practicable to determine disorder of written expression very early. This is because it is necessary for the child to have reached an age where it is expected that several types of writing will have been produced for comparison with that of others.

A child with disorder of written expression may be reluctant to write. He may have particular difficulty copying writing from the board, finding it easier to copy from material on his desk or table. The pupil may have an inconsistent handwriting style. Therefore the identification of such difficulties is likely to include: the pupil's approach to a writing task (e.g. reluctance); whether copying from the board appears particularly difficult; and the consistency of the child's handwriting style.

Regarding spelling, the pupil may have difficulties with: words ending in 'er', 'or' and 'ar'. He may spell 'paper' as 'papor' or 'papar'. The pupil may have problems with commonly used words as well as less frequently used ones; and sounds such as 's' and 'z'. The child may tend to: spell phonetically (e.g. 'fotograf' for 'photograph'); omit the middle or end of a word; spell certain words inconsistently ('nesesery', 'nececary', 'nesacary' and so on for 'necessary'); and write letters or syllables in the wrong sequence. Such difficulties are typical of pupils with dyslexia. It follows that the identification and assessment of a pupil's difficulty with spelling will include a profile of the sorts of errors made by the pupil in terms of the above characteristics.

Traditional and process approaches

It has been suggested that there are two broad approaches to teaching writing. These are: the traditional approach and the process (e.g. writers' workshop) approach (Pollington, Wilcox and Morrison, 2001).

The traditional approach tends to be skills based, involves sequential exercises and is teacher led. It may not be very motivating or interesting. The skills may not be generalised to the child's normal writing. At its least productive the traditional approach does not involve the teacher in teaching anything, only assessing the child's efforts. However, it has the advantage that it can produce steady progress recognised by the child, is predictable and secure. Also, in the hands of an enthusiastic teacher, skills approaches can be made stimulating and enjoyable.

Process approaches tend to emphasise the processes of composing writing and editing it. Manifestations are 'writers' workshop' (Morrow, 2001) and 'guided writing'. An example of strategies for using process approaches in the classroom is *Writing Through Childhood* (Harwayne, 2001). The child is not brought to believe that writing has to be exact as it is first produced. Rather he is encouraged to see writing as often passing through several stages before it reaches what could be called a finished stage. This is not intended as an inevitable approach. Indeed there are times when writing is well developed that requires the first attempt to be largely the final one. This is the case in examinations or in time pressured work situations.

Typical writers' workshop lessons are time structured. They involve teacher instruction, a section on an aspect of writing, then independent or group pupil work. Finally they involve sharing of the pupils' work in a plenary. Pupils see and learn from the teacher modelling how to offer constructive criticisms of work. They then work together commenting on each other's writing and acting as the audience for it.

Where the groups involve pupils with disorder of written expression, the teacher may need to provide extra support. This should enable the structure to work and ensure that the pupil with difficulties does not feel demoralised. As well as being used in a classroom setting, guided writing may be used in one to one remedial work. It involves the teacher modelling a particular strategy followed by the pupil (with guidance) applying the strategy or principle.

You will need to encourage the independence and peer interaction associated with a process approach. At the same time you will need to provide the structure for small steps to success that is often associated with basic skills methods. The use of the methods and their relative application can be informed by how well the pupil progresses and enjoys the lessons.

A parallel dichotomy can be found in approaches to teaching spelling. These centre on teaching spelling skills explicitly. This might involve using groups of words with similar sounds and endings such as 'fish', 'dish', and 'wish'. The spelling of words might be taught in context as they are needed for writing. As with the teaching of aspects of composition, each approach has strengths and weaknesses.

However, it appears it is particularly difficult for pupils with disorder of written expression to learn from only a contextual approach to teaching spellings. This is because the intensive practice that is needed to embed the spelling is rarely possible. The aspect of spelling that is likely to need support is the move from basic phonologically recognisable spelling such as 'cort' or 'cot' for 'caught'. The move is to the use of visual checking (does the word look right?) and spelling words based on one's existing knowledge of how other words are spelt.

Provision for writing and spelling

(a) Provision for handwriting

General

It is clear there are several aspects involved in the task of writing. It follows that there may be a range of ways in which writing can be improved and writing difficulties resolved.

Consequently, one principle of interventions for improving handwriting is that a focus on one of the 'underlying' difficulties will enable progress to be made.

For example, in copying a text, a pupil may find it difficult to co-ordinate movements in hand writing, while maintaining other aspects. These other aspects include retaining the visual memory of the words just read (in order to translate them into writing); and maintaining the sequence of different letters and words and translating these into written sequences.

The combination of skills may make it difficult for the pupil to concentrate on and improve one aspect such as co-ordination. If this is so, then it is assumed the associated skills (that is, the difficulties associated with them) can be approached distinctively. Also, to the extent that writing difficulties relate to difficulties with reading, interventions appropriate for reading problems may be suitable for problems with writing too.

Remediating sequencing

Indirect approaches to remediating sequencing difficulties might include tasks such as laying out sequences of bricks from left to right on a table. This will introduce the pupil to positional words such as 'before', 'after', 'next to', 'first' and 'last' and encourage him to use them. This positional understanding and the language linked to it may help the pupil begin to recognise a sequence of letters in a word, be able to talk about their position and reproduce this in writing.

The approach has logic to recommend it. It would be expected that understanding, talking about and trying to apply sequencing to words should help. But remember the approach is indirect and you will need to monitor the extent to which it leads to progress.

Improving co-ordination skills for handwriting

Teaching handwriting is also discussed in the chapter on developmental co-ordination disorder. In that chapter, the focus is on teaching handwriting to children with particular difficulties in motor co-ordination. The task is to teach and improve the co-ordination skills for writing. The main effort is on reducing the demands of the other sub skills of remembering and translating sequences of different letters from a page of print. It is maintained that this focus on reducing demands helps improve co-ordination for writing.

The task might be writing one repeated letter shape related to handwriting such as the following

ccccc
aaaaa
ggg

The early teaching of cursive script can help a pupil having difficulties with fine motor movements. This is because it is more flowing and controllable than forming separate letters. Also it enables the pupil to learn handwriting as it were in one go rather than having to learn to write in separate letters and then later change to cursive.

Handwriting may include problems with letter orientation and the reversal of letters. This is a common feature of many pupils when they are learning to write. If this is the difficulty, the correct formations may be taught directly. The pupil may begin with large letters, perhaps using a sand tray to aid orientation. The learner can be encouraged to look at the letter and say the letter as well as tracing it. Later the pupil will write the letter in a series on paper.

Teaching cursive script

Where letter formation for handwriting is taught using a cursive script, you may provide a chart to act as a reminder to the pupil of the shape of each letter. It is suggested (Pollock *et al.*, 2004) that a well-shaped letter 'c' is a good starting point. The individual letters should be written with an exit stroke so they can join other letters as follows:

cccc

This leads on to teaching the letters **aa, dd, gg** and **ee**. These units can then be the initial focus of practice in handwriting exercises even though other letters may be used in general writing. Other groups of letters can then be taught. The next group is the letters that determine the handwriting slant, such as **ll** and **jj**. Next are the letters that are a combination of curves and angles such as **bbb** and **fff**. Finally, the letters that can be formed in more than one way can be taught, for example **kkk** (Pollock *et al.*, 2004, pp. 109–11).

Compensatory tools for handwriting

There are several computer based strategies for bypassing handwriting problems. Pupils can use:

- a keyboard
- dictation with a voice recognition system
- word prediction programmes.

Each of these has been shown to improve the writing accuracy of pupils with learning disabilities (Lewis *et al.*, 1998). These tools do bypass handwriting difficulties. But as Berninger and Amtmann (2003, p. 351) point out the tools each have their own demands which a particular pupil with learning disabilities may or may not find challenging.

Keyboard skills might be thought to be an obvious alternative to handwriting. But a pupil needs to be able to automatically use the letter finding and keyboard skills involved in word processing. Otherwise word processing skills may not be fluent enough to be a viable alternative to handwriting.

Although dictation using a voice recognition system can eventually lead to better and longer text than a pupil may produce by handwriting, it is not a panacea. It still involves the pupil learning the commands for monitoring and correcting errors. He must be able to dictate, self-monitor for errors, and use the programme commands effectively. All this places considerable demands on working memory (Berninger and Amtmann, 2003, p. 352).

Word prediction software may also pose challenges for pupils having poor working memory or problems with attention or executive function because the pupil has to monitor the list of options that changes with each letter that is typed.

(b) Provision for writing composition

Framework for writing

Supporting frameworks for writing can help the pupil with disorder of written expression in several ways. They can be used to get the pupil started, give a sense of direction to the task and build confidence.

For example the teacher can encourage the pupil's understanding of the processes of developing ideas for writing, composing and editing. You can model the processes and use sets of questions that the pupil can later use to structure his own attempts. In generating ideas, the questions might be for a fictional story, 'Who is in the story?' 'Where does it happen?' 'What is the main thing that happens?' 'What happens, first, next, finally?' The pupil gradually takes on more of the task of generating ideas.

Similarly, the steps in composing the piece of writing can be modelled and gradually taken over by the pupil. In a non-fiction piece of writing where the ideas have been generated, the teacher can model the task of setting out the ideas in some kind of understandable order. Questions might be, 'What are the main ideas?' 'Which should come first?' 'What should come last?' Composition can then include taking each main idea in turn and expanding it into a sentence or two.

In editing, the teacher will show how she checks if the structure and shape of the piece of writing is good, whether paragraphs are used effectively, if grammar is clear, and if punctuation and spelling are correct.

Reducing task demands

To build confidence by providing initial success and to get a pupil started, reducing task demands can be useful. In story writing this can involve providing the beginnings of a series of sentences in a writing frame.

- When the light plane crashed, we found ourselves in the middle of the desert with no water and …
- All we could do at first was …

- Then we looked round the wreckage and noticed …
- So we made a …
- By nightfall it was …

You may wish to aid a learner's fluency in writing longer pieces of work and to save the pupil time using a dictionary for many words. If so you can provide key words that are likely to be used, or that the pupil indicates he wishes to use.

The underlying principle of reducing task demands is to enable the pupil to concentrate on smaller aspects of the overall task and improve on those. The teacher helps this by providing the structure for other aspects of the work so that the student completes a finished product. The initial focus might be on generating ideas, then composition, then editing and gradually the supports are faded out so that the pupil is able to carry out the whole process.

Software for essay structure

Software packages are available to help users develop and organise ideas, using diagrams to help. This allows ideas to be arranged, which can help with the structure of essays. Templates can be used for different subjects, including science and history. If a pupil is carrying out a piece of extended writing, such as an essay or research report, actively teaching the skills of how it should be presented is likely to be helpful (for all pupils).

More general software is also useful. Word processing packages are useful at different stages of writing a piece of work: planning, composition, checking and correcting and publishing. Talking word processors allow users to hear, through synthetic speech, the sentences they are typing as they are being typed. This can help reassure the pupil that what they are writing makes sense, and, where it does not, allows the pupil to go back and check accuracy. Once writing is completed, text can be highlighted and a tool used to hear a synthetic voice read the text.

Some programmes provide partial or complete sentences to support writing and allow the creation of personalised 'cloze' procedure exercises.

Note taking

Note taking is a complex and difficult skill. It is demanding for many pupils and where a pupil has difficulties with writing, demands are compounded. The pupil is likely to find it particularly difficult to concentrate on what is being said at the same time as keeping handwriting legible.

The teacher can encourage the pupil to write down only the key words. Then at the end of the dictation, the teacher gives the pupil a copy of her notes. The pupil goes through them highlighting the key words he has identified. The key words act as a revision aid and an anchor for reading the notes.

Writing for a purpose

As a motivational aid and as an incentive to produce work of good quality, writing for a particular purpose is helpful. The pupil may write a letter of thanks to a speaker who has visited the school. He may contribute to a newsletter about school events, or design and write a safety poster. The student may write to a pen friend, or send e-mails to pupils in other schools perhaps in different parts of the world. He may write shopping lists for class projects that involve buying items such as creating a school garden or organising a school fair. He may write to the local newspaper, apply for a job, write a story book for younger children in the school, write letters on behalf of elderly and infirm people in a local old people's home, or prepare a cooking recipe.

As well as being motivational such work of course provides invaluable opportunities for the pupil to consider the requirements of writing for different audiences. It is likely to be easier to judge the audience if the pupil initially writes to people whom he has met. These might be visitors to the school such as performers or speakers.

Developing self-regulation strategies

Pupils with learning disabilities tend to do little planning before they write and their approach tends to involve little monitoring and evaluation (Graham 1990). Their compositions are very short, with little detail or elaboration (Graham et al., 1991). One reason is their difficulty in sustaining the writing effort. In one study, fourth and sixth graders with learning disabilities were found to spend an average of only six minutes on writing an opinion essay. Yet with prompting, output could be considerably increased (Graham, 1990). Difficulties with the mechanics of writing such as spelling, punctuation and shaping letters also reduce content (Graham, Harris, McArthur and Schwartz, 1991). When pupils with learning disabilities do attempt revisions of their work, these tend to focus on mechanical aspects and neatness rather than compositional aspects of writing.

When given procedural support to ensure elements of the revising process were coordinated and occurred in a regular way, the revising of pupils with learning disabilities improved. Eighth grade students with learning disabilities were taught to make two passes through a composition. The first concentrated on global concerns such as there not being sufficient ideas. The second pass focused more on sentence level concerns such as a sentence not sounding right or an idea being incomplete. This produced better and larger revisions (De La Paz, Swanson and Graham 1998).

One approach to directly teaching pupils with learning disabilities to use the same types of strategies as more competent writers is 'self regulated strategy development' (see Graham and Harris, 2003, pp. 328–31 for a summary). It is an example of a cognitive strategies instruction model. This approach is intended to enhance students':

- strategic behaviours
- self-regulation skills
- content knowledge
- motivation.

One writing study (Sexton, Harris, and Graham, 1998) involved fifth and sixth grade students with learning disabilities. They had a difficulty with writing, low motivation and unhelpful beliefs about the causes of writing success and failure. The students were taught a *strategy* for planning and writing an opinion essay. It used steps to help them establish a goal for writing. Students created an initial outline for their paper (using basic components of thesis, supporting reasons, and conclusion). They continued the process of planning while writing.

The necessary *content knowledge* of the structure of an opinion essay was taught by defining the above basic components, identifying them in essays by others, and generating ideas for each component. Students were helped to *regulate* their use of the strategy. To achieve this, the teacher modelled how to use it while thinking aloud, using self-statements such as 'What do I need to do?' and 'Did I say what I believe?' Teacher and students discussed these self-statements and students were praised when they later used them in learning the strategy. Motivation and unhelpful beliefs were also directly tackled.

(c) Interventions for spelling

Multi-sensory aspects

There is a range of approaches using multi-sensory aids to teach spelling (Pollock *et al.*, 2004). In teaching early letter sounds, the teacher can include the first letter of the child's name, say, 'p'. Other letters might be 'm' for 'mum'/'mom', 't' for 'tiger' and 'a' for 'apple'. Words are chosen that have a personal interest for the child and which can be illustrated and visualised. These are taught as the sound the letter makes rather than the pronunciation of the letter name (e.g. 'a' pronounced as in 'cat' not as in 'cape').

The teacher talks with the child about the letter sound and shape using cards on which the letters are written in front of them. This leads to basic word building with words like, 'pat' and 'mat' depending on the first few letters that have been introduced. In the approach, 'simultaneous oral spelling', the pupil says the letters as he writes them. This helps link kinaesthetic memory and auditory memory.

Visual recall can be aided by the teacher showing the pupils a written word and asking them to concentrate on the word and remember as much as possible about it. After removing the word from view, the teacher prompts with questions such as, 'How many letters in the word?' or 'Were any of the letters the same?' to encourage visual recall.

The auditory recall of words can be encouraged by games such as clapping out the syllables of the word. Or you can ask the students to group words according to their sound, as with, 'dog', 'bog', 'log' and so on. Rhymes, poems and songs of course help highlight the sounds of words. A child with auditory difficulties might not hear the similarities of words taught in clusters to aid spelling ('wish', 'dish'). Consequently, the teacher will need to make sure that the common rhyme, 'ish' is noticed.

Simply looking at words does not seem to be enough for most learners to be able to learn how to spell a word (Graham, 2000). The contribution of kinaesthetic, speech motor and auditory senses are necessary. In the early stages of learning to spell (and in learning to read) phonemic awareness is important (Torgesen and Mathes, 2000). This enables the different sound units of the word to be linked to the graphic representation.

Multi-sensory work for writing and spelling draws on speech–motor, kinaesthetic, visual and auditory memory. Large letters may be drawn using the finger in a sand tray so that the shape and sequence of letters is emphasised. Smaller letters may then be traced, leading to the writing of letters on paper. Having the child say and sound out the word (for phonetically regular words) may further embed this. This brings in speech–motor memory as the child articulates the word. It also involves auditory memory as the child hears the sounds.

Often, a reading disorder appears to be related to a difficulty with phonological processing. In such instances the teacher can work on teaching and supporting better phonological awareness in conjunction with letter-sound instruction. This would be expected to contribute to improved spelling.

The 'look-cover-write-check' approach is familiar to many. Drawing on other senses too the strategy can be extended to 'look-say-finger trace-cover-write-check'. This can include the strategy of looking at the word shape overall as well as looking at individual letters. This is important given that the words where this approach is used are not normally phonetically regular words that can be guessed from knowing their sounds.

Directed Spelling Thinking Activity

In the Directed Spelling Thinking Activity (Graham, Harris and Loynachan, 2000), a group of pupils study words in a particular way. They are helped to contrast, compare and categorise two or more words according to their finding similarities and differences in them. The aim is to raise awareness of spelling patterns and more complex grapho-phonological principles.

Let us assume that students are examining words with a long /i/ sound as in 'thigh', 'by' and 'pie'. They are encouraged to discover that the long /i/ can be made by the letters 'igh' as in not only 'thigh' but also in 'sigh'. It can be made with the letter 'y' in 'by' but also in 'try' and 'cry'. The long /i/ can be made by 'ie' as in 'pie' and in words such as, 'lie' and 'die'.

The pupils are encouraged to classify other similar words into groups or notice that they do not follow the common principle. Consolidating activities might be looking at a piece of writing in which examples of the words conforming to the rule appears. As the teacher, you will have previously checked to ensure this is the case. It has been suggested this approach is used with pupils with 'learning disabilities' (Graham, Harris and Loynachan, 2000). A similar approach, 'word sort' has been used with 'delayed readers' (Zutell, 1998).

Target words

Target words may reflect the recommendations for spelling programmes (Tiedt, Tiedt and Tiedt, 2001). That is they include high frequency core words, personal words, and patterns words illustrating some morphological or phonological principle. The personal words will include a list prepared with the pupil. These will be words used often in the week in various contexts. Of course some of these may be high frequency core words also. Groups of words can be made in consultation with older students and subject specialist teachers. These would comprise words often needed in the subjects, for example in science or geography.

When the pupil works on words that have been misspelled in free writing sessions, the words to be worked on will reflect the school's spelling policy. This strategy is likely to be most helpful when it involves selecting only a few misspelled words from a piece of work. These may be words which are very commonly used.

While repetition of spellings is a necessary aid, effort should be made to generate interest in the tasks involved. Short daily activities with weekly checks of progress are better than long drills. Games, puzzles and computer activities so long as they focus on the important words can be motivating and helpful. Software is available that allows the user to decide how words are grouped and to add words of the user's choice. Games and strategies to improve spelling may be included.

Other software employs a 'look-cover-write-check' approach to learning spellings. The words are in 'families' or subject groups. Personalised lists can also be made. Sometimes, remembering the spelling of target words can be made easier by using visual mnemonics and word associations (Mercer and Mercer, 1998). A pupil who often misspells 'piece' as 'peice' might find the phrase 'a piece of pie' a useful reminder of the letter order.

Alternative and augmentative communication

In another book in this series, *The Effective Teacher's Guide to Autism and Communication Difficulties (2nd. Edition)* is a chapter on 'Communication disorders: speech'. It considers alternative and augmentative communication.

This section briefly touches on the relevance of alternative and augmentative communication to written communication through symbols and related matters. Symbolic communication involves the use of symbols such as a word or a picture to stand for something. 'Non aided' communication involves the child making a movement or vocalisation that does not necessitate a physical aid or other device (Vanderheiden and Lloyd, 1986). 'Aided' augmentative communication involves using a device or item such as a communication board, eye gaze board and electronic systems.

Three categories may be identified (Bigge, Best and Wolff Heller, 2001, p. 237):

- non-electronic devices
- dedicated communication devices
- computer based communication systems.

Non-electronic devices may be communication boards and communication notebooks. Communication books can include photographs, symbols and words. These enable a pupil to find a symbol and show the particular page to someone who may not know the symbol. The recipient viewing the page can then see the intended word.

Dedicated communication devices are electronic communication systems that speak programmed messages. These messages are spoken when the user activates locations marked by symbols.

Computer based communication systems may consist of a computer with input options, communication software, and a speech synthesizer. Computer aided communication may involve the pupil having a voice production device with a computer based bank of words and sentences. These words and sentences are produced by pressing the keyboard keys. Symbols may be part or whole objects used to represent an item or activity. Often what is meant when people refer to symbols is a system of graphical communication. In this system, each symbol represents a concept such as an object, person, activity or attribute.

Communication grids in which several symbols are set out in a specified order can enable a pupil to participate in group sessions. They can be used to support the retelling of a story. A sequence of symbols can be used to indicate a sequence of activities, including a school timetable for a pupil. Computer technology, using symbols, allows the pupil and the adult to use a large number of symbols flexibly. There are symbol e-mail programmes, and websites that use symbols.

Curriculum and assessment; pedagogy; resources; therapy/care; and organisation

Curriculum and assessment

Given the centrality of writing to many school subjects, attainment in these may be lower than is age typical where written responses are required. Remember the knowledge in the subjects may be the same as for other children. The balance of subjects may emphasise writing to encourage and support progress in this.

Planning across the curriculum will help ensure that other subjects and areas work to support literacy. As explained earlier key words may be identified that will be explained and reinforced in certain subjects such as science or geography.

Small steps of assessment may be used to recognise progress in written expression and spelling.

Pedagogy

Approaches for disorder of written expression include: remediating sequencing, improving co-ordination skills, teaching cursive script, frameworks for writing, reducing task demands, and support for note taking, and self-regulated strategy development. To improve spelling, interventions may involve multi sensory approaches, Directed Spelling Thinking Activity, and target words.

Resources

Among resources used for disorder of written expression is computer software to help with essay structure. Where graphical symbols are used the relevant resources are required.

Therapy/care

There appears to be no distinctive therapy necessary for disorder of written expression. Where there are co-ordination difficulties affecting writing a physical therapist/physiotherapist and an occupational therapist may work with the teacher to devise programmes to improve co-ordination.

Organisation

There appears to be no distinctive organisation of the school or classroom necessary for disorder of written expression. However, as a supplementary approach to more direct interventions such as self regulated strategy development, aspects of classroom environment have been identified.

These involve developing an environment conducive to the development of self regulation such as encouraging pupils to share their writing with others; securing classroom routines where planning and revising are expected and reinforced; and a classroom ethos that is supportive (Graham and Harris, 1997).

Thinking points

Readers may wish to consider:

- how the tensions between essential skills learning, which may lead to observable progress, and the use of learning in context, which may be more meaningful, are reconciled;

- how the effectiveness of the strategies mentioned above will be assessed for a particular pupil to help ensure they are helping progress;
- how links between the teaching of writing and the teaching of reading and speaking and listening will be inter related so each enhances the others.

Key texts

Fletcher, J. M., Lyon, G. R., Fuchs, L. and Barnes, M. A. (2007) *Learning Disabilities: From Identification to Intervention* New York, Guilford Press

Drawing on genetic, neural, cognitive and contextual information, this book considers classification, definition, identification and assessment and intervention for disabilities. The disabilities considered are in: reading (word recognition, fluency, comprehension), mathematics disabilities, and written expression.

Gunning, T. G. (2002) (2nd Edition) *Assessing and Correcting Reading and Writing Difficulties* Boston, MA, Allyn and Bacon

This is a very practical book with ideas and lesson plans for helping with reading and writing. The second chapter looks broadly at a range of reasons why reading and writing difficulties can occur.

Chapter 4

Developmental co-ordination disorder/dyspraxia

Introduction

This chapter presents a definition of developmental co-ordination disorder and looks at estimates of its prevalence. I consider possible causal factors. The chapter examines developmental processes considered to underpin developmental co-ordination disorder (gross and fine motor co-ordination, and perceptual-motor development). I look at ways of assessing developmental co-ordination disorder. Turning to provision the chapter outlines aspects of the curriculum; pedagogy; resources; therapy/care and organisation.

Definitions

At a consensus meeting held at the University of Western Ontario in 1994 participants agreed on the preferential designation developmental co-ordination disorder, to refer to children with developmental motor problems in accordance with American Psychiatric Association (2000, pp. 56–57) criteria. It was an attempt by researchers to bring consistency to the literature to help evidence based practice. Despite this a number of terms continue to be used in describing and diagnosing children with developmental motor difficulties. Neither has a universally agreed set of characteristics been identified for these children (Ahonen *et al.*, 2004, pp. 269–70). This inconsistency in definition relates to the hetero-geneous nature of the group of children considered to have developmental co-ordination disorder and its different manifestations.

There is debate about the definition of developmental co-ordination disorder and related matters. One area of debate concerns the extent to which there may be subtypes of the condition. A related area of discussion is the extent to which it is helpful to consider developmental co-ordination disorder in the context of a variety of learning problems such as reading disability, specific language disabilities and attention deficit hyperactivity disorder (Dewey and Wilson, 2001, pp. 40–53).

Definitions are affected by the way provision is made. In the United States of America, the term 'dyspraxia' is still widely used and is not considered an exactly equivalent term. Developmental co-ordination disorder is not considered a learning disability in the United States of America but many children might receive services within the education system based on the impact on academic performance.

In the United States of America and in Canada provision for health care and for education is made differently. In Canada, it also differs by province. In Canada developmental co-ordination disorder is not considered a learning disability from an education perspective. However some parents have been able to acquire special education identification under the umbrella of learning disability because of academic impact or under the physical disability umbrella if the child demonstrates self-care or safety concerns at school. A child can receive accommodations in school in the form of an Individualised Education Plan without having formal identification if a health condition is identified. There is an argument for having developmental co-ordination disorder recognised as a disability that usually requires differentiated instruction and accommodation (Private communication, C. Missiuna, McMaster University, Ontario, 2010).

A widely used definition is that agreed by the American Psychiatric Association. Developmental co-ordination disorder is considered a 'marked impairment of motor co-ordination' which 'significantly interferes with academic achievement or activities of daily living'. It is 'not due to a general medical condition' (American Psychiatric Association, 2000, pp. 56–57).

Developmental co-ordination disorder is not associated with any medically evident neurological signs. This helps distinguish it from cerebral palsy and other conditions affecting motor co-ordination but in which there are overt neurological symptoms. (See also Cermak, Gubbay and Larkin, 2002 pp. 2–22). The expression 'clumsy child syndrome' was more commonly used previously. This expression conveys something of a common feature of developmental co-ordination disorder or at least a possible subtype (Cermak and Larkin, 2002).

The term 'dyspraxia' (from the Greek, 'difficulty in doing') continues to be used in some countries and among some professionals. Where this is so, definitions tend to focus on the planning and organisation of movement. Dyspraxia is sometimes seen as a sub type of developmental co-ordination disorder. Dyspraxia has been defined as a 'marked impairment in gross and fine motor *organisation* (which may or may not influence articulation and speech) which are influenced by poor perceptual regulation.

These difficulties present as 'an inability to *plan and organise purposeful movement*' (Dixon and Addy, 2004, p. 9, italics in original). It appears the child knows how to carry out activities but has difficulty organising movements to accomplish them. Nevertheless, dyspraxia still relates fundamentally to motor actions (see also Cermak and Larkin, 2002, pp. 42–46). Developmental verbal dyspraxia is a speech difficulty. This is considered briefly in the book in this series *The Effective Teacher's Guide to Autism and Communication Difficulties* (2nd. Edition) in the chapter 'Communication disorders: speech'.

There are several characteristics of the motor performance of children with developmental co-ordination disorder: these are slower movement time; relying more on visual information than on proprioceptive information; and inconsistency in some aspects of motor performance in relation to other skilled movement. Related but more cognitive aspects include the child's failure to anticipate and use perceptual information and benefit from cues; and failure to use rehearsal strategies (Dewey and Wilson, 2001, p. 18, paraphrased).

More generally, children tend to show difficulties with gross and fine motor skills in terms of both speed and accuracy. This is owing to motor control and co-ordination problems as well as difficulties with sequencing movements. It is important that you as a teacher and others note the amount of effort and time it takes a child to perform a task as well as whether or not he can perform it (Cermak and Larkin, 2002).

Prevalence and co-occurrence

Estimates of prevalence of developmental co-ordination disorder vary widely from 6 per cent to 22 per cent. This is thought to be influenced by the assessment procedure and the background experience of the assessor (Kirby and Drew, 2003, p.52). Related to difficulties estimating prevalence (and definition) is the complicating issue of the degree of co-occurrence of developmental co-ordination disorder with other conditions, the exact nature of which is debated (Martini, Heath and Missiuna, 1999).

Gillberg (in Landgren *et al.*, 1998) identified 589 children aged 6–7 years in a Swedish community considered to have some form of neurological disorder. Of the children identified as having Deficit of Attention and Motor Perception, all had developmental co-ordination disorder and attention deficits. About half fulfilled the criteria for attention deficit hyperactivity disorder. Kaplan and colleagues (1998) noted an overlap between developmental co-ordination disorder, attention deficit hyperactivity disorder and dyslexia. They found 23 per cent of a diagnosed group having all three conditions.

Possible causal factors

The causes of developmental co-ordination disorder are not fully known. Never the less evidence points to the problems of children with developmental co-ordination disorder being multi-dimensional. No single factor has been identified as a direct cause. This could support the use of multi-causative models to understand the interconnections between genetic predisposition, brain structure, prenatal influences and postnatal effects (Cermak et al., 2002).

In the aetiology of developmental co-ordination disorder, there is debate about the relative importance of motor and of nonmotor factors. 'Nonmotor' refers to the processing of perceptual information in the service of action. 'Motor' concerns control processes responsible for selecting and programming an appropriate motor response taking account of environmental input (Wilson and McKenzie, 1998).

It has been proposed that influential nonmotor factors, in relation to developmental co-ordination disorder, include:

- visuoperceptual deficits
- visuospatial representation deficits
- deficits in kinaesthetic function
- deficits in visuomotor integration (Wilson, 2005, p. 292).

A meta-analysis of developmental co-ordination disorder literature (Wilson and McKenzie, 1998) has been carried out. This suggested the main deficit associated with developmental co-ordination disorder was visuospatial processing irrespective of whether a motor response was required or not. Kinaesthetic perception, especially where active movement was involved was an important factor. So was cross modal perception involving different modes such as visual and movement perception. It has been argued that deficits in the visuospatial representation of *intended* movements may be an important part of the explanation of motor clumsiness in children (Wilson, 2005, p. 293).

An aspect of analysis of deficits in motor control involves studying how children make reaching movements to objects or targets in space. Children with developmental co-ordination disorder and other children without the disorder are compared in relation to the temporal and spatial characteristics of their movements. Reaction time, movement time, movement accuracy, and movement variability are studied. This is to try to determine how children with developmental co-ordination disorder plan, organise and carry out motor responses. Studies of goal-directed arm movements have examined the ability of children with developmental co-ordination disorder to use visual and kinaesthetic feedback for movement control (Pryde, 2000).

Such studies suggest that characterising the effects of developmental co-ordination disorder on manual aiming has to take account of the requirements of the aiming task. Important aspects are whether the child is allowed to see his hand movements, the size of the target, and the amplitude of movements. It has been argued (Roy et al., 2004, pp. 54–55) that overall, developmental co-ordination disorder does not affect the initial programming of movement. It does however affect the processing of feedback information and the integration of feedback from vision and proprioception. Never the less for some children, earlier programming stages do appear to be affected.

Developmental processes considered to underpin developmental co-ordination disorder

Fundamental to a child being able to plan and perform co-ordinated actions is that he correctly interprets incoming sensory information from the environment. Three key systems provide information to enable the development of co-ordinated and controlled movement: the sensory, proprioceptive, and vestibular systems.

In the present context, the sensory system refers particularly to the senses of sight, hearing and touch and is sometimes taken to include the proprioceptive and vestibular systems too.

The proprioceptive system provides information concerning where the limbs are in relation to the rest of the person's body without him having to look (Estil and Whiting, 2002, p. 71).

This involves receptors within the joints and muscles that monitor the stretch of muscles and indicate the position of each limb (Dixon and Addy, 2004, p. 15). For a child with developmental co-ordination disorder this information may not be as acute as it is for other children. Certain activities may be particularly difficult including dressing where many buttons are involved, and wiping the bottom after using the toilet. Gross motor movement is difficult and consequently the child may be heavy footed.

The vestibular system involves receptors in the inner ear sending impulses to the brain to assess the position and movement of the head relative to the rest of the body. This is important for balance and the sense of movement including velocity. Children for whom this system is dysfunctional tend to lack control of the speed of their movements. Also a child with developmental co-ordination disorder tends to have problems maintaining balance, that is poor equilibrium, and may therefore be afraid of movement.

As well as affecting fine and gross motor movement, the sensory, proprioceptive and vestibular systems influence visual and auditory perception. Interrelated elements of perceptual-motor development that are affected include:

- visual–motor co-ordination
- visual form constancy
- spatial position
- spatial relationships.

Where proprioception, vestibular feedback and sense of touch are not as acute as is typical, *visual-motor co-ordination* (eye–hand co-ordination) is affected. The proprioceptive system provides inaccurate and slowly processed information about where the arm and hand are positioned and about how much movement is required to reach an object. Visuo-spatial judgement is therefore influenced, impairing fine motor control.

Visual form constancy involves being able to recognise that an object that may appear different is still the same object. For example, the object may be in a different position from when first encountered. In the process of a child developing a mental map of an object and coming to recognise it as a 'category', touch is an important aid. A child with developmental co-ordination disorder may get incorrect information about an object because of a dampened sense of touch. Therefore he is unable to absorb important tactile cues about the object. A clear mental schema of the object is not developed. The child may have difficulty developing form constancy, having to rely excessively on the sense of vision to help.

Acquiring a notion of one's *spatial position* enables one to perceive depth in space; to perceive body position relative to surroundings (e.g. above or below); and develop a body schema and a realistic body image. Many learners with developmental co-ordination disorder have a poor sense of position in space. Consequently they have a poor understanding of self-image, a poor appreciation of body proportions, and a lack of understanding of laterality. The latter can lead to difficulties locating left and right and more generally, poor orientation. The child may avoid crossing the body mid line by turning the body so that the left hand can pick up an item on the child's right without the left arm crossing the body mid line. The child's writing might be 'mirror' writing and letters in words might be reversed. Map reading will be very difficult.

Turning to *spatial relationships*, to understand these, the child has to be able to perceive the position of two or more objects in relation to one another and in relation to him. This in turn depends on developing adequate form constancy, position in space, and figure-ground discrimination. Because a child with developmental co-ordination disorder has problems assessing space and judging distance, he tends to have difficulties with activities such as negotiating his way to the front of the class, or climbing stairs. He is likely to have difficulties with physical education activities like climbing wall bars, or vaulting.

In writing, the size of letters may be variable and spacing between letters either excessive or insufficient. Columns for mathematical calculations may be inconsistent, causing errors. Activities such as crossing the road will be problematic and require adults to take great care when making judgements about a child's safety. Please see also the chapter 'Development of the Child' (Kirby and Drew, 2003, pp. 27–50).

Identification and assessment

A multi professional assessment of developmental co-ordination disorder will provide a range of useful information. It may involve the physician (who may make the initial diagnosis), physical therapist/physiotherapist, and occupational therapist. Other professions contributing will be the school psychologist, speech pathologist where there are language implications, and the teacher.

When tests are compared that aim to assess developmental co-ordination disorder, they do not always consistently identify children as having or not having developmental co-ordination disorder (Crawford *et al.*, 2001). This suggests that information from standardised tests along with an assessment of functional performance may increase accuracy of identification. Observation and assessments based on professional judgement also contribute.

Assessment is also informed by the assessor being aware of possible characteristics. A child around 4 or 5 years old with developmental co-ordination disorder may find it more difficult than others of the same age to go up and down stairs. He may learn to use the toilet independently much later than peers, and may have difficulty handling toys and performing tasks requiring dexterity such as completing jigsaws.

A child around 5 to 11 years old with developmental co-ordination disorder might find it hard to generalise skills because they are not secure or automatic. Most pupils developing typically will find tasks such as adapting to catching various balls of different sizes pose little difficulty. For the pupil with developmental co-ordination disorder adapting for such activities will be almost like learning a new skill each time. The child may also be accident prone, tending to knock things over or bump into objects.

Older students may be disorganised. They may find it difficult to move around a large high school/secondary school and get to lessons on time. This will especially be the case if there are stairs to negotiate or if the building is on a large site or several sites.

For older and younger pupils, particular school subjects such as art, science and design and technology pose their own challenges. In some subjects, safety implications loom large. For example, where hazardous substances are handled, the school will need to make pupil specific risk assessments. Developmental co-ordination disorder poses particular difficulties for handwriting, physical activities, and social and personal development (Cermak and Larkin, 2002, passim).

Provision

Curriculum and assessment

The overall levels of curriculum are likely to be broadly similar to that of children without disorders/disability. However, there will be particular care developing the curriculum in areas where motor co-ordination is central. These include handwriting, physical education, art, geometry and aspects of social and personal skills development. Also implicated are subjects where it is necessary to use tools such as craft or technology; and laboratory work, for example in biology, chemistry or physics. The balance of subjects is likely to reflect this with an emphasis on those areas where the child needs extra practice and support.

Components within subjects that require coordination may also be emphasised for example handwriting in English studies. Assessment may be finely grained in the areas of motor development to ensure students' progress is monitored. Small steps of assessment also indicate to the student and the teacher that some progress has been made so this can be recognised and celebrated.

Pedagogy

In general, pedagogy related to developmental co-ordination disorder includes identifying tasks that are difficult for the child and breaking them into smaller steps, so-called task analysis. This is so they may be easier to teach and to learn. These steps are taught in contexts where their usefulness is apparent. The activity may be adapted and/or equipment used to enable activities to be accomplished.

Handwriting

A difficulty with acquiring handwriting skills for a child with developmental co-ordination disorder is the challenge of learning the motor plan or programme of the letters. This is made difficult because of problems in motor planning or spatial orientation. Additionally, the child may have problems with forming letters correctly and legibly because of motor control deficits.

A child with developmental co-ordination disorder may adopt a poor writing posture because of proprioceptive difficulties. The pupil is more likely to adopt a better posture if the chair and desk height are correct. They should produce a ninety-degree angle between the line of the upper body and the line of the upper leg, and a similar angle between the upper and lower leg and the knee.

The position of the paper to be written on is important but the pupil with developmental co-ordination disorder may misjudge this because of spatial difficulties. A sheet of paper should be aligned with the child's arm. Marking on the child's desk or the use of a large card template will help ensure this is maintained (Benbow, 2002, p.271).

For a pupil with developmental co-ordination disorder, developing a good pencil grip may prove difficult. Because of poor tactile sensation the child may grip tightly so as to feel the pencil better. Fluency may be further affected by poor proprioceptive sense in the joints of the fingers and hand. The muscles in the hand may be underdeveloped or muscle tone may be poor. This is likely to hinder the fluency and comfort of writing, impair legibility and cause fatigue.

Pencil grip is improved by the pupil using the preferred hand. Most children have a preferred hand by the age of seven years although for children with developmental co-ordination disorder it may be older. A three-cornered pencil grip or a pen with a rubber finger grip can help. Proprioceptive feedback may be improved by specific tasks aimed at enhancing dexterity.

The pressure of the pencil on paper may be too light or too heavy because of proprioceptive difficulties affecting co-ordination and exerting pressure. Physical tasks can be used to temporarily boost limb awareness. The effects typically last about forty minutes before further exercises are necessary. One exercise is performing up to five repetitions of rotating horizontally held arms beginning in small spirals that are gradually increased. The student then reverses the direction and reduces the spirals from large to small (Addy, 2004).

A pen that illuminates when pressed for writing can help the pupil become more aware of pressure exerted when writing. A pupil tending to press too lightly will be encouraged to make the implement light up. By contrast, a child tending to press too heavily will be encouraged to avoid illuminating the pen.

Where a pupil has difficulty with eye-hand co-ordination he will find it hard to place the pencil on a particular point, an essential skill for writing. This can be tackled by encouraging increasingly refined movements of the hand and fingers, then of placing a pencil point. The pupil can begin by placing a finger on a marked area of paper. Gradually the area is decreased so it is a spot. Next the pupil is asked to perform a similar series of tasks but using a pencil, eventually placing a pencil point on a specified dot (Dixon and Addy, 2004, pp. 66–80).

Adequate form constancy is essential. This is because a central part of handwriting involves: recognising, identifying and distinguishing shapes and different sizes of shapes; and reproducing shapes, correct in form and size. To help, multi-sensory approaches may be used to develop the child's experience and understanding of shapes and sizes. Soft clay material may be manipulated to make different letter shapes. When a pencil is used, the child may make lines (horizontal, vertical, diagonal) and basic shapes (circle). A diagonal line is likely to be particularly difficult for a pupil having problems with laterality because it necessitates simultaneously crossing from left to right and from top to bottom.

The child can work on more recognisable pre-writing patterns to help develop the rhythm and fluency necessary for writing. When the child is taught to write letters of the alphabet, it can help to get the correct shapes if special lined paper is used. This has a central line and a line above and below. The upper line indicates the height of the ascending letter and the lower line signifies the depth of the descending letter. It helps if letters are taught with joins/integral exit strokes to aid learning of cursive script (Dixon and Addy, 2004, pp. 66–80).

Turning to movement control, the child has to learn the forms of letters and how they join cursively. Because of processing difficulties, the child may have difficulty stopping a letter. He may run the line of a letter on so that, for example, a 'c' has a bottom tail that is far too long. The pupil will need to learn that the letters have a beginning and an end. This can be helped by providing some practice writing a series of letters in a specified short horizontal line in which the start and finish are marked by vertical lines. Because of difficulties with laterality and orientation, pupils with developmental co-ordination disorder often reverse letters. The student may write 'b' for 'd' and 'p' for 'q' at an age when most students do not. This can be remedied by emphasising the writing of letters grouped according to whether they are formed by using a clockwise or an anticlockwise motion (Dixon and Addy, 2004, p.76).

- Letters formed with a clockwise motion are 'b', 'h', 'j', 'm', 'n', 'p' and 'r';
- Those shaped with an anticlockwise motion are 'a', 'c', 'd', 'e', 'f', 'o', 'q', 't', 'u', 'v' and 'w';
- Ones requiring both motions are 'g', 's' and 'y'.

Kinaesthetic aids tend to help the pupil's visual orientation of the letter. You can ask the pupil to write letters in the air and guide his movements as necessary. Teaching cursive script from an early age tends to help with letter orientation. Pupils with developmental co-ordination disorder tend to space letters and words poorly because of poor spatial organisation. To help, cursive writing can be introduced early and the pupil can be encouraged to leave a finger space between words. This works best when using pencil rather than pen which may smudge.

Benbow (2002, p. 269) suggests several reasons for favouring cursive writing. The patterns of movement better enable more automatic motor learning. Reversing and transposing letters is less likely. The connected line helps the learning of words as units. Also, writing is faster because the child does not have to start and stop as he does when printing letters.

Fluency in writing is difficult to attain for a child with developmental co-ordination disorder. Moving from pre-writing patterns to the formation of letters with joins/integral exit strokes to cursive writing can assist the pupil's fluency. The pupil is not taught to write 'separate' letters. A kinaesthetic approach, perhaps using a sand tray for writing letters, helps the child develop a mental image of the letter forms and how they link together. Commercial writing programs may also be used. Other programmes include the cursive programme Loops and Other Groups (Benbow, 1990) and the pre cursive programme by Clough (1999). Benbow (2002, pp. 248–79) has summarised aspects of hand skills and handwriting.

Physical education

It can raise self esteem if the child finds some success in physical education. Bundy (2002) suggests a child may be participating in games and activities with other children but may not be getting as much enjoyment. Also, as children with developmental co-ordination disorder are likely to be less competent, they may be less accepted by peers. This can lead to feelings of isolation and low self worth.

For a child with developmental co-ordination disorder, physical activities pose a challenge. Skipping with or without a rope may be difficult. Riding a bicycle is a complex task for anyone. It involves balance, co-ordination and constantly processing and responding to visual information for steering. For a child with developmental co-ordination disorder, having difficulties with co-ordination, spatial difficulties and poor judgement of speed, it is hardly surprising the skill of learning to ride a bicycle is delayed.

In physical education lessons, spatial difficulties will make it hard for the child to move about among apparatus. Difficulties judging distance and velocity will make many ball games very challenging. With high school/secondary school students some co-ordination difficulties may be less noticeable, as many other students will be going through a clumsy period because of the adolescent growth spurt.

In the United States of America, 'Adapted Physical Education' is an individualised programme provided by people who have studied the requirements of physical education instruction for children with disabilities. The Adapted Physical Education teacher concentrates on fundamental motor skills and physical performance of individual pupils. She may work with pupils for a certain number of designated hours per week (Gabbard, LeBlanc and Lowry, 1994). The classroom teacher and the Adapted Physical Education teacher can work productively together to develop and teach programmes of physical education as well as leisure and recreation. This relates to pupils with developmental co-ordination disorder and to other pupils, for example those with health or orthopaedic impairments.

A pupil with developmental co-ordination disorder may see a physical therapist outside school time. However there is scope for innovative work when the teacher of physical education and a physical therapist work together. They can plan and implement physical education lessons to include pupils with developmental co-ordination disorder.

Black and Haskins (1996) suggest ways activities can be structured to enable all pupils to participate in physical education lessons. This can be assisted through:

- parallel activity
- inclusive adapted activity
- discrete adapted activity.

Using the example of ball skills, in a *parallel activity*, pupils play a game together but in their own way using different strategies to reach the same learning goal. To develop the skill to send and receive a ball, pairs of pupils having acquired this skill can pass the ball while moving and from several metres apart. Others still developing the skill can pass while stationary and be closer to each other.

An *inclusive adapted activity* involves games and activities that are adapted so all pupils can participate. For older students, a game of volleyball can be adapted using a light sponge ball allowing more time for students lacking advanced skills in relation to the game to position themselves and reach the ball. Students adept at the game will tend to enjoy such variations occasionally because the changed timing of skills creates a different element of challenge.

In a *discrete adapted activity*, pupils take part in pairs or practice individually. In developing skills for a game in which a bat is used to strike a ball (e.g. soft ball) a pupil with developmental co-ordination disorder may practice using a larger bat or a lighter ball.

A related approach to developing adaptations with reference to pupils with physical, health or multiple disabilities is to use adaptive words to act as a guide to help select and design suitable adapted physical activities. These include 'increase or decrease' which may involve increasing rest periods between sections of a game or decreasing the length of time for each segment of a game. 'Reduce or enlarge' suggests reducing the dimensions of a game such as having a smaller volleyball court or enlarging goals for a game of soccer. 'Raise and lower' might indicate raising the number of attempts allowed to successfully carry out an activity. This might be raising the limit on three strikes and out in a kickball game or lowering the balance beam in gymnastics (Bigge, Best and Wolf Heller, 2001, pp. 474–75).

As indicated, a pupil with developmental co-ordination disorder may find physical education lessons daunting. Having a space for each pupil to which they may return (for example in gymnastics) can help provide a sense of predictability and security that is reassuring. Floor markings can be used to indicate the paths the pupils are expected to follow. This will help the child with developmental co-ordination disorder with orientation and direction. Changing for physical education and changing back into day clothes afterwards in the limited time usually allowed is difficult. Adapted clothing using false buttons and Velcro fasteners can help. Parents and the student are likely to choose or adapt such clothing. It is best if it is fashionable or at least does not draw the wrong sort of attention.

Personal and social development

Pupils with developmental co-ordination disorder can become frustrated and demoralised and come to have low self-worth. This is partly because of the persistent difficulties they face that may not always be understood by others. Such feelings may emerge in the form of difficult behaviour. In these circumstances you as the teacher and others will try and establish the root cause of the behaviour. The more you understand developmental co-ordination disorder and the greater your skills in supporting a pupil with developmental co-ordination disorder the better. Then there is a greater likelihood that the pupil will be able to deal with the challenges of education and other day-to-day demands.

Several difficulties associated with developmental co-ordination disorder influence the development of social skills. Motor perceptual difficulties can make it difficult for the child or young person to realise they may be standing too close to a conversational partner. Because of spatial and orientation problems, the pupil may have a poor appreciation of his own body language. He may be insufficiently aware of the importance of and subtlety of gesture and body position. Gesture may be poorly co-ordinated with speech and the pupil may be unaware of other people's non-verbal signals, missing the clues that facilitate smooth communication.

Poor co-ordination may inhibit participation in social activities such as dancing, ice-skating and bowling. Using public transport and finding one's way after asking directions may be hindered by orientation difficulties. Handling small coins can be problematic, particularly if under time pressure as when in a store at the front of a busy line.

At mealtimes, younger pupils with developmental co-ordination disorder may have difficulty co-ordinating a knife and fork. They may spill liquids and may take a long time to finish eating a meal. Cutting food may be particularly difficult (Hoare, 1994). In preparing a meal, activities such as using a can opener and buttering bread may be tricky. A wall can opener and cutlery with thick rubber handles are possible adaptations.

Moving about without bumping into people or knocking into or knocking over objects may be difficult in itself. Co-ordination difficulties hamper involvement in team games requiring high levels of motor co-ordination, such as football, some computer games and board games. This limits opportunities to socialise and participate.

Some social skills can be taught using established behavioural techniques. The teacher can use positive reinforcement of student's behaviours approaching what is desired. Or you can use social learning methods such as modelling. One approach is having the adult model appropriate behaviour followed by the pupil engaging in role-play to practice the skill. You might model standing an optimum distance from someone one does not know well when speaking.

Both personal hygiene and personal appearance can influence peer acceptance. Children with developmental co-ordination disorder may have difficulty with washing hair, cleaning teeth, and cutting fingernails (Gubbay, 1985). For younger pupils, using the toilet may be problematic. This is because wiping the bottom involves spatial and proprioceptive skills as the part of the body concerned is out of view. Also, for girls, unless the technique of wiping the bottom with a movement towards the back is learned, there is a risk of urinary infection.

False buttons above Velcro fasteners on clothing, and trousers with an elasticised waist can save time dressing and undressing for the toilet. This is an important factor if the child wishes to use the toilet in the allocated recess times without being late back for lessons. Wet wipes rather than dry toilet tissue can clean the bottom more thoroughly and easily. A small foot rest by the toilet can be useful for younger pupils so that the legs are not dangling down and the child does not have to hold on to the sides of the toilet to keep balance. A mirror behind the door of toilet cubicles will allow the child with developmental co-ordination disorder to see himself when dressed to check he is tidy.

In high school, hygiene may still be problematic. Girls may find changing sanitary products very difficult. They may find it hard to apply make-up sparingly, requiring sensitive guidance from parents and the school. Please also see a chapter on daily living skills and developmental co-ordination disorder by May-Benson, Ingolia and Koomar (2002, pp. 140–156).

Resources

Aids to more fluent writing include pencil grips and illuminating pens as described above. Special equipment for physical education may be used such as extra light balls and extra large bats. Adapted equipment may be used such as cutlery with thick rubber handles. False buttons above Velcro fasteners may be used on clothing, and trousers may have an elasticated waist.

Therapy/care

Since developmental co-ordination disorder affects activities of daily living, the occupational therapist can assist the child in their daily life activities. Such activities are organisational skills, dressing, and school activities such as handwriting.

A pupil with developmental co-ordination disorder may see a physical therapist outside school time. As mentioned earlier, there are good opportunities for innovative work with the teacher of physical education and a physical therapist or occupational therapist working together. The work of therapists indicates aspects of the debate about provision and its effectiveness centring around so called 'bottom up' and 'top down' approaches.

Bottom up approaches involve attempts to remediate supposed underlying motor deficits, which is expected to lead to improvements in motor performance. Among bottom up approaches are sensory integration (Ayres, 1989); process orientated treatment (Laszlo and Bairstow, 1985); and perceptual motor training (meta analysis by Kavale and Mattson, 1983). In summarising evaluations of these approaches, it has been suggested (Mandich *et al.*, 2001, p. 61) that no one approach or combination of approaches 'is superior to another in improving motor skill'. Also, none 'has been shown to be reliably better than no treatment at all' (ibid.).

Top down approaches include: task specific intervention involving direct teaching of the task to be learned (Revie and Larkin, 1993) and cognitive approaches, which include 'cognitive orientation to daily occupational performance' (Polatajko, Mandich, Miller and Macnab, 2001). Cognitive-behavioural techniques employ various methods enabling children to demonstrate suitable motor responses. The therapist provides positive reinforcement of approximations to the desired responses and their successful performance. This helps the child subsequently initiate his own movements. It is rather early to make judgements about the efficacy of top down approaches as they are relatively new, but initial indications look promising.

For example, Cognitive Orientation to Daily Occupational Performance developed for children with developmental co-ordination disorder (Polatajko, Mandich, Missiuna, *et al.*, 2001) typically involves an occupational therapist working closely with parents and the child. It aims to help children discover the particular cognitive strategies that will improve their ability to carry out everyday tasks such as handwriting, riding a bicycle, using cutlery and catching a ball.

Cognitive Orientation to Daily Occupational Performance employs global and domain specific strategies and the guided discovery of strategies. These enable the child to achieve goals he has selected. 'Dynamic performance analysis' is used to try to determine when a child has difficulties performing an activity. This enables performance breakdown to be identified. The therapist teaches the child a global strategy called 'Goal-Plan-Do-Check' to act as a framework for solving motor based performance problems.

The therapist then guides the child to discover domain specific strategies to enable the activity to be performed (Polatajko and Mandich,

2004). A review of a series studies indicates that Cognitive Orientation to Daily Occupational Performance shows promise as an effective means of promoting skill acquisition and transfer in children with developmental co-ordination disorder aged 7 to 12 years (Polatajko, Rodger, Dhillon and Hirji, 2004, p. 461).

Organisation

The teacher's physical organisation of the classroom can help the child by ensuring relatively free movement around the room without unnecessary clutter. The child may sit close to the front of the class in a seat near to the entry door to avoid bumping into other children and objects.

Ideally the classroom will be large enough for different furniture arrangements for different activities such as group work or whole class work to be laid out permanently. This allows the child with developmental co-ordination disorder to become accustomed to the layout rather than have to constantly adapt as furniture is moved into different arrangements for different activities. However, space may be at a premium and stable layouts may not be possible. In this situation, the positions into which furniture is moved for different activities can be marked on the floor of the classroom so that the positions are predictable and consistent.

Thinking points

Readers may wish to consider:

- how effective approaches that will help pupils with developmental co-ordination disorder are across all areas of school life and in particular subject lessons;
- how teachers, teaching assistants and others can work more effectively with physical therapists and occupational therapists to enhance overall provision.

Key texts

Cermak, S. A. and Larkin, D. (2002) *Developmental Coordination Disorder* Albany, New York, Delmar Thompson Learning

Parts of the book successively concern subtypes and conditions that co-occur with developmental co-ordination disorder; assessment; mechanisms underlying the condition; functional implications; and interventions.

Kirby, A. and Drew, S. (2003) *Guide to Dyspraxia and Developmental Coordination Disorders* London, David Fulton Publishers

A readable overview, this book includes separate chapters focusing on the younger child, the adolescent, and the adult.

Missiuna, C. (Ed.) (2001) *Children with Development Co-ordination Disorder—Strategies for Success* New York, Haworth Press

The chapters of this coherently presented book progress from seeking to define developmental co-ordination disorder, identifying the condition, considering evidence for various treatment approaches, and looking in particular at Cognitive Orientation to Daily Occupational Performance.

Sugden, D. and Chambers, M. (2005) *Children with Developmental Coordination Disorder* London, Wiley

Intended for researchers and various professionals, this book links research findings and clinical work to inform practice.

Chapter 5

Mathematics disorder/dyscalculia

Introduction

This chapter considers definitions of mathematics disorder and looks at its prevalence. I examine causal factors; and the identification and assessment of mathematics disorder. Provision is then described in terms of teaching prerequisite skills, general approaches, mathematics difficulties relating to developmental co-ordination disorder, and mathematics difficulties relating to reading disorder.

In the final section the chapter summarises provision in relation to curriculum and assessment; pedagogy; resources; therapy/care; and school and classroom organisation. An example of an Internet site giving a brief overview of mathematics disorder is (www.schwablearning. org/articles).

Definitions

Mathematics disorder is sometimes called dyscalculia although the two terms are not always exactly equated. The preference in the present book is for the term 'mathematics disorder'. This is to avoid the potential medicalising of problems with mathematics through the use of a Greek word that sounds rather like an illness. It can still be argued that even the use of the expression, 'mathematics disorder' makes difficulty with mathematics unjustifiably into a 'disorder'.

However, where the term mathematics disorder is used, it usually refers to a level of difficulty with mathematics far beyond what might be expected with typically developing children. To this extent the implication is that there is a 'within child' element. The difficulties cannot be easily laid at the door of poor teaching or lack of opportunity. Below I examine definitions for both mathematics disorder and for dyscalculia.

Mathematics disorder is considered to be a difficulty in understanding and learning mathematics that is not associated with general cognitive difficulties. In the *Diagnostic and Statistical Manual of Mental Disorders Fourth Edition Text Revision (DSM-IV-TR)* (American Psychiatric Association, 2000, p. 53) the essential feature of mathematics disorder is mathematical ability falling substantially below that expected for the child's chronological age, intelligence and age appropriate education. The disorder 'significantly interferes' with academic achievement of daily living that requires mathematical skills.

'Dyscalculia' is defined in a document relating to a national numeracy strategy in England as:

' ... a condition that affects the ability to acquire mathematical skills. Learners with dyscalculia may have difficulty understanding simple number concepts, lack an intuitive grasp of numbers, and have problems with learning number facts and procedures. Even if they produce the correct answer or use the correct method, they may do so mechanically and without confidence' (Department of Education and Skills, 2001a).

Notice that the particular definition of 'dyscalculia' considered does not specify the level of difficulty as clearly as does the definition provided by the American Psychiatric Association.

A pupil with mathematics disorder may have difficulty performing simple calculations such as addition. He may have difficulty knowing how to respond to mathematical information. The pupils may substitute one number for another or reverse numbers (e.g. 2 for 5). He may misalign symbols for example when using a decimal point; and name, read and write mathematical symbols incorrectly.

Attempts have been made to identify and delineate different 'types' of mathematics difficulty and these extend and supplement basic definitions.

- *Spatial dyscalculia* relates to difficulties in visuo–spatial assessment and organisation.
- *Anarithmetria* involves confusion with arithmetical procedures, for example, mixing written operations such as addition, subtraction and multiplication.
- *Lexical dyscalculia* (alexia) concerns confusion with the language of mathematics and its relationship with symbols (e.g. subtract, take away, deduct, minus, and '−').
- *Graphic dyscalculia* refers to problems with being able to write the symbols and digits needed for calculations.
- *Practographic dyscalculia* is characterised by impairment in the ability to manipulate concrete objects or graphically illustrated objects. The child has difficulty in practically applying mathematical knowledge and procedures and may be unable to arrange objects in

order of size, compare two items according to size, or state when two items are identical in size and weight (Senzer, 2001).

Some of these purported types of mathematics disorder appear to be related conceptually to either dyspraxia or dyslexia. For example, spatial dyscalculia may relate to dyspraxic difficulties. Lexical and perhaps graphic dyscalculia may relate more to dyslexic difficulties. (Jordan and Hanich, 2003; Jordan, Hanich and Kaplan, 2003)

Prevalence

The prevalence of mathematics disorder is difficult to determine because it is not always regarded as a separate entity. Definitions as shown in the definition in English guidance (Department of Education and Skills, 2001b) are not always precise enough to be relevant.

Often mathematics disorder is associated with reading disorder or developmental co-ordination disorder and interventions are developed within that context. Also, the level at which difficulties with mathematics are sufficiently severe to constitute a disorder is not always agreed.

It has however been estimated that about 6 per cent of students have significant difficulties learning basic mathematical concepts and skills (Fleischner and Manheimer, 1997). Regarding arithmetical disability, estimates taking into account studies in the United States of America, Europe, and Israel suggest that 5 per cent to 7 per cent of school age children show some form of arithmetical disability (Geary, 2003, p. 200).

Causal factors

In this and subsequent sections mention is made of certain brain structures (for a technical description, please see Standring, 2005). This section refers to the parietal lobe. The cerebrum (Latin 'cerebrum' = 'brain') comprises the cerebral hemispheres, associated with thinking, communicating, and carrying out skilled, co-ordinated tasks. Each cerebral hemisphere can be divided into four lobes, named after overlying bones, each lobe being associated with a certain type of cognitive functioning. They are the frontal, temporal, parietal and occipital lobe. The parietal lobe is important for attention and for interpreting sensory information, being the destination for sensors in skin and joints conveying information about touch and position.

Foetal alcohol syndrome has been associated with babies being born with the parietal lobes underdeveloped. These are considered important for numeracy. Underdevelopment of the parietal lobes is associated with the child later having difficulties with mathematical cognition and number processing (Kopera-Frye *et al.*, 1996).

Different neural systems contribute to mathematical cognition, one of which is a verbal system (Dehaene *et al.*, 1998). This appears to store, as well as verbally rote learned information, number facts such as number bonds. The system underpins counting and numerical rote learned knowledge like multiplication tables. Consider a child with mathematics disorder who also has reading disorder. If the reading disorder has a phonological basis, then the neural system affected may be the verbal system underpinning counting and calculation (Goswami, 2004, p. 179).

Another neural system concerned with the representation of number appears to underpin knowledge concerning numbers and their relations (for example one number being larger or smaller than another) (Dehaene *et al.*, 1998). Located in the intraparietal areas of the brain, the system is activated by such tasks as number comparisons (whether using numerals, words or clusters of dots). Visuo-spatial regions may be involved with complex calculations (Zago *et al.*, 2001) where visual-mental imagery may be important. A particular parietal-premotor area is activated during finger counting and calculation (Goswami, 2004, p. 179).

Identification and assessment

In identifying mathematics disorder, you will need to bear in mind the definition of mathematics disorder and its possible characteristic difficulties. The identification and assessment of mathematics disorder is also informed by other difficulties the pupil may have. For example, if the pupil is identified as having reading disorder or development co-ordination disorder, the mathematics disorder is assessed in those contexts.

Among commercial assessments is the computer-based *Dyscalculia Screener* (Butterworth, 2004). This is for children aged 6 to 14 years, and measures pupils' response times and response accuracy. Typically, a score lower than the twentieth or twenty-fifth percentile on a mathematics achievement test and a low average or higher IQ score are considered to indicate arithmetical disability (Geary, Hamson and Hoard, 2000). However, interpreting the detail of the tests and monitoring progress are important.

In curriculum terms, the pupil will be assessed to establish the gaps that exist in his mathematical knowledge and skills. This diagnostic approach will inform what is taught (Silver and Hagin, 2002). Good assessment will also influence the pace at which mathematics is taught, the contexts, the amount of support needed from concrete apparatus and other matters.

Provision

This section takes a pragmatic view looking at teaching prerequisite skills; general interventions and approaches; approaches relating to developmental co-ordination disorder; and approaches relating to reading disorder. Prerequisite skills are those relating to classification, number, length, area, volume, weight, and position and movement. General interventions and approaches consist of reducing anxiety, using concrete experience, and adapting and applying knowledge and mathematical problem solving.

Teaching prerequisite skills

The development of subsequent skills and understanding necessary in mathematics is hindered if there is not a secure basis of certain prerequisite skills:

- classification
- number
- length
- area
- volume
- weight
- position
- movement.

Classification begins with very simple distinctions such as 'same' and 'different'. It extends to more sophisticated classifications such as grouping shapes with the same number of sides and angles. To help a pupil recognise patterns of relationships and recognise groups (e.g. groups of objects of the same colour) you can provide practical experience of and practice in classifying. You begin with easy classifications and make them gradually more complex.

Number sense has been variously defined but may be taken to include: being able to subitise small quantities (that is rapidly, accurately and confidently judging number given a small number of items); recognising number patterns; comparing numerical magnitudes; estimating quantities; counting, and carrying out simple number transformations (Berch, 2005).

If a pupil is having difficulty with number, it is helpful to check that certain precursors such as the following are in place and to teach them using practical examples and experience if they are not. The pupil may struggle with concepts relating to 'more' or 'less'. He may have difficulty learning that one number has a greater value than another (e.g. 5 and 3). There may be difficulty relating size and quantity. For example, the learner may not know that five tiles laid out on a flat surface will take up a smaller space than ten tiles of the same size arranged similarly. The pupil may find it hard to estimate an answer before working a problem out.

He may confuse the direction in which things get bigger and smaller. One source of this confusion may be the apparent illogicality of numbers in a sequence and numbers representing values. In a number line (1, 2, 3 ...), numbers to the left are progressively smaller in value. With digits, the value to the left is bigger in the sense that it represents tens, hundreds etc. (e.g. in '24' the '2' on the left represents '20') (Poustie, 2001b, p.71).

Difficulties with place value may relate to numbers being misread so that the correct information is not used. The difficulties may concern numbers being miswritten, in which case the pupil may know the correct answer to a calculation but miswrites it. Problems with place value may concern not understanding the concept, perhaps because of difficulties in understanding the language used. To rectify any mistakes relating to place value it is important you ask the pupil to explain his working out. The correct remediating strategy can then be determined.

A precursor to understanding *length* such as the length of a line is grasping that length is 'conserved' even when the line is bent or curved. A pupil having difficulty with this notion would be shown two straight pieces of wire and recognise they were the same length. If one of the pieces of wire were then bent (say into an 'S' shape) the pupil would not recognise or accept it was still the same length as its partner. He may assume length has to do with the length of the space the wire occupied (which is smaller when the wire is bent) rather than being a retained property of the wire. To rectify this, you can provide plenty of experience that length stays the same by very gradually bending the wire and having the pupil agree it is the same length as before then progressively bending it a little more.

In order to understand *area*, it is necessary to be able to match circumscribed areas. For example the pupil should be able to match two squares of identical areas from several squares with different areas. This can be taught directly, giving the pupil plenty of experience of matching area visually. Initially, the pupil can be given a square and a choice of two other squares only one of which matches the pupil's square. Subsequently, the number of squares can be increased. Later still, the learner can be asked to match two squares from several laid out on the table, so he has to identify both squares.

To begin to understand *volume*, the pupil has to realise that volume is conserved even if the container of the substance is different in size and/or shape. The pupil should be given plenty of practical experience using liquids and containers of different sizes and shapes. A rather obvious point but one that can confuse a pupil in the early stages of understanding is to take care not to spill the liquid. Only then can it be demonstrated that the volume of liquid remains the same.

Among precursors of understanding *weight* is that the pupil grasps the conservation of weight. He has to understand that, if two malleable items weigh the same and one is then made into a different shape, it will still weigh the same as its partner. To teach this, the pupil might begin by reading his weight on scales when standing. He can then check the reading when crouching to show that weight is constant. This develops into weighing items and changing their shape and then weighing them again to confirm their weight is the same (Poustie, 2001b, pp. 22–23).

Consider a pupil with difficulties regarding *position and movement* in mathematics. Early work can involve the pupil developing an understanding of his own position in relation to other objects. He might be asked and if necessary guided to stand 'in front of' a box, 'beside' a box, 'behind' a box and so on. The pupil would later direct another person into similar positions to give the pupil practice in using the correct expressive vocabulary.

General approaches

Reducing anxiety

Some students become anxious when expected to demonstrate competence applying mathematical skills (Battista, 1999). Sometimes difficulties with attention are exacerbated by stress and anxiety about doing mathematics.

Reassuring the pupil and trying to make mathematics enjoyable, perhaps using games, can help reduce anxiety and help the pupil relax and therefore concentrate and attend better. Where anxiety about mathematics is high, individual tuition can help ensure early success and reduce the anxiety of not getting the task right.

Where anxiety about mathematics is part of a severe level of anxiety more generally, psychotherapeutic approaches may be used but these are beyond the scope of this chapter. Approaches to anxiety disorders may be found in another book in this series *The Effective Teacher's Guide to Behavioural and Emotional Disorders: Disruptive Behaviour Disorders, Anxiety Disorders and Depressive Disorders, and Attention Deficit Hyperactivity Disorder (2nd. Edition).*

Concrete experience

Using concrete apparatus helps give the pupil experience and understanding of what is being done and a pupil with mathematics disorder may require consolidation using concrete items longer than most pupils. Even when more abstract methods are being used, concrete reminders can still be helpful for some tasks. Number lines or a box of physical shapes that are labelled are examples.

Concrete material such as Dienes MAB blocks, Stern's equipment and Unifix blocks are useful in developing understanding of computation and other mathematical understanding. Cuisenaire rods are useful physical aids using size and colour to help pupils' understanding of many aspects of mathematics (Poustie, 2001b, pp. 61–63 gives many practical ideas).

Westwood (2000, p. 41) accepts that structural apparatus 'provides a bridge between the concrete experience and abstract reasoning by taking learners through experiences at intermediate levels of semi-concrete … to the semi-abstract'. He also gives a timely reminder that such apparatus is by no means foolproof in helping pupils acquire understanding. The pupil may not connect activities carried out using the apparatus with the mathematical concepts you want to convey, so you will still need to discuss with the pupil the task and assess his understanding.

Adapting and applying knowledge and mathematical problem solving

The pupil may find it difficult to adapt existing knowledge, finding it hard to dispense with procedures unsuited to the task in hand. Consider a pupil physically adding to six existing items different numbers of items, (e.g. two, three, four). The pupil may count from one every time instead of adapting the counting approach and counting on from six.

Regarding generalising mathematical skills, the pupil may learn an approach in one situation with one set of items. But he may not apply the approach in another situation with other items when most other children would do so. Plenty of practice and application in other contexts can help embed mathematical concepts and terms.

How do you help a pupil apply and adapt mathematical learning such as being able to count money to practical situations like spending money in a shop? For this, structured practice of different teaching strategies and practice in using them can be helpful. Similarly, the pupil may be taught to apply approaches and skills to different situations. Applying knowledge can be helped if you first ensure the skills are very

secure. Then you can gradually introduce the extra demands of applying the knowledge and skill in different circumstances. Using money for
shopping can begin with buying a single item with a known price using
the exact amount of money, allowing the pupil to cope better with the
social demands of shopping. Later the task can be made increasingly
complicated by requiring change and buying several items.

Related to the issue of generalisation arising in connection with
adapting and applying knowledge, is the development of the ability to
carry out mathematical problem solving. Fuchs and Fuchs' (2003)
research programme indicated that for pupils with mathematics disabilities, a strong foundation in the rules of problem solving was
necessary. Children had to master solution methods on problems with
'low transfer demands'. These were problems that were worded the
same as previous problems and in which only quantities and the cover
stories were different.

After this foundation, it was possible to progress to problems with
higher transfer demands. These require transfer to problems with certain
differences making it more difficult to recognise the problem that is
already known. Also explicit instruction on transfer was needed aimed
at increasing the child's awareness of the connections between new and
familiar problems. This was achieved in two ways. The first way was
by broadening the categories by which pupils group problems that
require the same solution methods. The second way was by prompting
pupils to search novel problems for these broad categories (increasing
metacognition) (ibid. p. 318).

Mathematics and developmental co-ordination disorder

Recall the underlying difficulties associated with developmental
co-ordination disorder and some of the approaches suggested in relation
to handwriting in the chapter on developmental co-ordination disorder.
Bearing these in mind, it is possible to understand why certain difficulties
arise in mathematics and how they might be tackled.

Number

Many students with learning disabilities have difficulty learning and
recalling number facts and tables (Ostad, 1999). A student with developmental co-ordination disorder may have difficulties with fine motor
co-ordination, eye-hand co-ordination and spatial relationships. If so, he
may have difficulties writing numerals, for example getting the size correct.

Squared paper with squares of a size allowing the child to write a number in each can help the child get the size of numerals more consistent. It has also been suggested that numerals can be taught in groups that avoid teaching very similar numerals that may be confused (3 and 5; 6 and 9). The groups would be introduced as 1, 2 and 3. Particular care is taken that 3 is formed and practiced before 5 is introduced. Next, 4, 5 and 6 would be taught with care that 6 is practiced before 9 is taught. The next group would be 7, 8, 9 and 10 (El-Nagar, 1996).

If spacing between numerals is excessive or insufficient, or columns for calculations inconsistent so that errors are made, squared paper can help. Difficulties with orientation may make it hard for the pupil to follow and reproduce the sequence of a calculation from left to right or from top to bottom. This can be explicitly taught. The pupil would be reminded of the direction of the calculation by arrows of a different colour to that used for the child's calculations. These arrows are inserted at the beginning of a horizontal sum and at the side of a top to bottom calculation as indicated below:

$$\rightarrow 6 + 7 = 11 \qquad \begin{array}{l} 6+ \\ 7 \downarrow \\ \hline \end{array}$$

Also, difficulties with motor co-ordination may lead to a symbol being incorrectly written or copied. The student may write 'x' for '+'. If therefore a pupil writes '5 + 2 = 10' this may indeed reflect an incorrect calculation. But it might indicate the pupil was trying to write '5 x 2 = 10'. It is important that place value is securely understood and where this is achieved, mistakes are reduced.

More generally, it is essential to ask the pupil to explain the working out so such misunderstandings come to light. Marking a calculation incorrect is little use to the pupil if the reasons for a mistake are not explored and remedied.

Space, shape and measure

Because of such difficulties as orientation, the pupil with developmental co-ordination disorder may have problems with positional words such as 'up', 'down', 'behind' and 'in front'. The pupils may have difficulties understanding and using positional words and phrases and linking them to different aspects of spatial relationships. These positional words need to be explicitly taught and linked with practical experience of the positions they convey.

You might begin by applying the words to the position of the pupil's body, for example teaching the pupil positions such as standing 'behind' a tree or 'in front' of a tree. Miniature models are then used. A figure could represent the pupil and a model could represent the tree. The pupil manipulates these to develop and confirm understanding. Next, two-dimensional representations are used. These could be immediately observed digital photographs (of the pupil standing behind/in front of the tree) and drawings.

Regarding shape, the pupil having difficulties with form constancy may not see shapes accurately. Consequently, when the learner is required to reproduce them from memory he will have difficulties replicating the correct form and size. This will be exacerbated if the pupil has difficulties with fine motor co-ordination. In this instance he will find it hard to draw the shape even if he had visualised it accurately. Problems with laterality tend to make it hard for the pupil to draw shapes involving diagonals. This is because the lines involve negotiating two sets of directions: left–right and up–down.

To help a child recognise shapes, you can encourage him to handle and explore physical shapes such as a square or triangle. Multi-sensory approaches can help especially kinaesthetic and tactile methods to encourage the accurate reproduction of shapes. An example is drawing shapes in a sand tray or making them from a soft modelling material. The child may struggle to understand symmetry because of problems identifying left and right.

This can be taught through games in which the child's body is the first indicator of what is left and right (not the teacher's left and right as she faces him). With his own left hand and right hand marked in an agreed way, the child is asked to go to his left or right. With a group, the game, 'Simon Says' can be a vehicle for introducing and practising this. Later, looking at a shape that can be handled and which has a clear line of symmetry, the pupil is asked to show the left and right of the shape. Drawings of shapes can then be used to check the pupil understands the concept and to teach and reinforce it further.;

How can you help a pupil recognise three-dimensional shapes and drawings of such shapes and draw a three-dimensional shape? You can provide plenty of guided opportunities for the pupil to handle and talk about three-dimensional shapes. A structured programme can be used in which the child is introduced to two-dimensional representations of three-dimensional shapes while the latter are present. This can help the pupil begin to recognise and match the aspects of the three-dimensional shape and the representation.

Turning to weight, pupils with poor proprioception, whose muscle receptors are not as sensitised as most other children, have difficulty understanding weight. The pupil will benefit from being provided with structured experience of handling objects of different weights. Terms such as 'heavy', 'light', 'heavier than' and 'lighter than' need to be learned and understood.

The pupil is introduced to measuring weight using a balance where respective relative weights are indicated by the position of the balance. The notions of 'heavier than' and 'lighter than' are refined in this way. Spring scales can be introduced later. For linear measuring, where a pupil has difficulties with fine motor co-ordination, a ruler with a small handle on the flat broad side can be used.

Mathematics and reading disorder

It appears that reading and language capabilities enable young children to compensate for deficits in certain areas of mathematics. The reading and mathematics achievement and particular mathematical competencies of seventy-four children were tracked over second and third grade. Children were initially classified into one of four groups:

- moderate mathematics deficiencies but normal reading achievement;
- moderate mathematics deficiencies and moderate reading deficiencies;
- moderate reading deficiencies but normal mathematics;
- normal mathematics achievement and normal reading achievement.

Many of the children were not eligible for special educational services, their disabilities being relatively mild. The group with 'moderate mathematics deficiencies but normal reading achievement' and the group with 'moderate mathematics deficiencies and moderate reading deficiencies' both started out at the same level in mathematics. The former group passed the latter over time. Children with moderate mathematics deficiencies (whether or not they had reading deficiencies) tended to be weak in fact retrieval and estimation. The group with moderate mathematics deficiencies and normal reading performed better at problem solving than did the group that had deficiencies in both mathematics and reading (Jordan and Hanich, 2003).

Other relationships between reading disorder and mathematics disorder may be considered with regard to apparent underlying difficulties. Difficulties with reading disorder discussed in an earlier chapter included:

- phonological difficulties;
- auditory perception and auditory processing difficulties;

- short-term verbal memory difficulties;
- sequencing difficulties (temporal order).

Similar difficulties are considered below in relation to mathematics problems for the pupil with reading disorder.

Phonological difficulties and auditory perception and auditory processing difficulties

It has been suggested (Geary and Hoard, 2001) that there may be a relationship between deficits in processing sounds (a feature of reading disability) and accessing arithmetical facts from long-term memory. Certainly, learning number facts involves counting, which involves number words and the use of the phonetic system. But it is therefore unclear why children with mathematics disability only who presumably have intact phonetic abilities, also demonstrate deficits in fact retrieval (Jordan, Hanich and Kaplan, 2003, p. 834).

It is important that the teacher's use of language in explaining mathematical relationships corresponds to the student's comprehension level (Cawley *et al.*, 2001). More specifically, difficulties with phonological representations and with auditory processing and auditory perception may make it hard for the pupil with reading disorder to develop a secure understanding of the language of mathematics. The pupil may have difficulty in acquiring and using mathematical language such as 'addition', 'place value', 'decimals' and 'fractions'. Perhaps he has limited experience of mathematical vocabulary receptively and expressively.

Using mathematical language correctly complements developing the understanding and skills with which the language is associated. You can introduce and explain new words and display key words throughout the lesson, for example on a board. Wall displays with key words as their focus can be built up as new words are introduced.

Number stories aim to give the pupil a better understanding of word problems and how they are constructed (Poustie, 2001b, pp. 33–34). The pupil might make up and tell a story about '3' and '7', perhaps that there were seven children in a camp in the forest. Three of them went out to explore and three were left. The pupil would then be encouraged to write the different sums that could be made from the story such as '7 − 3 = 4'. This can be a real confidence builder for a child who has struggled with terms such as 'subtract' and 'minus'. It can help develop the language necessary to picture and understand some of the principles at work in basic arithmetic.

Potentially misleading language may require explanation and examples. The fact that the numbers in 'twenty three' are said with the 'tens' part of the number first but the 'fourteen' is said with the units part of the number first can confuse some children. How can you help deal with this anomaly? You can provide a careful explanation with examples of the expression 'teen' meaning 'ten' and the rule that for numbers thirteen to nineteen, the number is said in this way.

Difficulty with working memory

Difficulties with short-term verbal memory may be apparent in the pupil having difficulty with remembering: numbers, multiplication tables, or the sequences of a mathematical operation. If a pupil has difficulties remembering numbers, this can be helped by his using concrete items to help the pupil retain the numbers mentally. If necessary this can be supplemented by one-to-one tuition. Memorising multiplication tables can be helped by table grids. These use visual patterns such as having some of the numbers coloured. This allows the learner to combine the use of visual sense as the pupil scrutinises the grid and auditory sense as he or another person says the numbers.

To help the pupil remember instructions and sequences of numbers, multi-sensory approaches (including allowing the pupil to talk through a calculation) are useful. Also helpful is regular practice and over-learning, though not to the point of boredom. Mnemonics can help such as SOHCAHTOA to remember the relationships for sine (opposite over hypotenuse), cosine (adjacent over hypotenuse) and tangent (opposite over adjacent).

In mental mathematics, the pupil may have difficulty retaining the necessary information and simultaneously processing it to calculate the solution. You might make only one part of the task mental allowing the pupil to write down the key number and the sign for the mathematical operation. For the problem 8x9, the pupil would write down 8x and remember the 9 mentally then work out the calculation mentally.

Physical aids to memory such as number lines and multiplication squares can assist calculations. Visualising may help the pupil deal with otherwise abstract problems. The calculation, 9+7 = 16 would be visualised as 'I have nine books and I get another seven books making sixteen'. Some symbols can be remembered better with a visual clue. The signs < and > are easily confused. However, they can be remembered as crocodile teeth with the mouth open more widely for the bigger number. This is easier to remember than '8 < a' means 8 is smaller than 'a'.

Sequencing difficulties

Effective planning often rests on the pupil knowing the sequence in which the tasks need to be done. Where this poses difficulties, careful explanations and step by step guidance are important. Mind Maps ™ allow information including sequences to be presented visually. They may help the pupil with planning and organisation.

Normally, calculations for x, − and + involve working from right to left. This is the case in the calculation below. You begin on the right adding the five units and the three units. Then you move to the left to add the 1 ten and the 8 tens.

$$15\ +$$
$$83$$
$$\overline{}$$
$$98$$

But when dividing, you work from left to right. This is illustrated in the calculation below. You first divide the 8 tens by 2. Then you move to the right to divide the four units by 2.

$$2\overline{)\,84}$$

Sequences of numbers, 1, 2, 3, 4 and so on, may be taught in small steps. This is so that the pupil will first learn the sequence 1, 2 securely, then 1, 2, 3 and so on over several sessions as necessary. Time sequences, such as the days of the week and the months of the year, can similarly be explicitly taught and practised using multi-sensory aids. These aids might include pictures or photographs associated with different days. Again the sequence can be learned in small steps. An example of teaching the sequence of numbers on an analogue clock face (which also relates to constructional difficulties) was provided in the chapter on 'Reading disorder'.

Curriculum and assessment, pedagogy, resources, therapy/ care, and organisation.

The structure of the chapter in the context of prerequisite skills, general approaches and with regard to developmental co-ordination disorder and reading disorder was a presentational device. It now remains to reinterpret what has been said so far in the chapter in relation to the curriculum and assessment, pedagogy, resources, therapy and care, and school and classroom organisation. The approach to mathematics disorder is through these aspects of provision.

Curriculum and assessment

Attainment in mathematics will be lower than age average. Levels of the curriculum may be lower than age typical in areas where mathematics is a major component. Such areas include physics, chemistry, biology, and geography.

The balance of subjects may emphasise mathematics so that progress can be encouraged and supported. Within subjects the mathematics elements will be highlighted for support. Small steps of assessment may be used to demonstrate progress in mathematics. This enables the student who is struggling to see that progress is being made.

Pedagogy

Pedagogy includes the explicit practically orientated teaching of prerequisite skills; and general approaches such as providing extensive concrete experience. It embraces approaches relating to developmental coordination disorder such as help with the alignment of number calculations. Pedagogy also includes approaches relating to dyslexia, for example support for phonological difficulties and mathematics language.

Resources

There appear to be no distinctive resources essential for mathematics disorder beyond the use of concrete materials suitable for all children. However the extent of the use of these resources is likely to be greater for students with mathematics disorder. The duration over which students may require the help afforded by such resources is likely to be longer than is age typical.

Therapy/care

There appears to be no distinctive therapy essential for mathematics disorder. Where anxiety concerning mathematics appears severe, then psychotherapy may be useful and this may be in the context of wider anxiety disorder.

School and classroom organisation

There is converging evidence that explicit systematic instruction with numerous opportunities for students to respond and to talk through their thinking is helpful to students with mathematics disorder (Gersten et al., under review). See also the Instructional Research Group, California (www.inresg.org).

Therefore classroom and group organisation that facilitates this is likely to aid learning. Opportunities for small group discussions and for pupils to speak with partners is likely to be helpful if well focused.

Thinking points

Readers may wish to consider with reference to a particular school:

- the extent to which there is effective provision for the prerequisites to mathematics;
- the effectiveness of general approaches used;
- the degree to which there is suitable provision for mathematics difficulties related to developmental co-ordination disorder and reading disorder;
- how these approaches are rationalised into a comprehensive and coherent set of interventions;
- how effectiveness of the overall provision is monitored and improved.

Key texts

Campbell, J. (Ed.) (2005) *Handbook of Mathematical Cognition* New York, Taylor and Francis.

A collection of chapters by researchers into the cognitive and neurological processes underlying mathematical and numerical abilities.

Chinn, S. and Ashcroft, R. (2006) (3rd. edition) *Mathematics for Dyslexics, Including Dyscalculia* London, Wiley

Written with a United Kingdom context in mind, this book provides information on dyscalculia, research evidence and resources.

Dowker, A. (2005) *Individual Differences in Arithmetic: Implications for Psychology, Neuroscience and Education* New York, Taylor and Francis.

Reviews research into areas including arithmetical abilities, causes of arithmetical difficulties, and interventions.

Westwood, P. S. (2000) *Numeracy and Learning Difficulties: Approaches to Teaching and Assessment* Melbourne, Australian Council for Educational Research.

This book examines the various ways students acquire mathematical skills and suggests flexible methods of teaching to accommodate these. Problem solving strategies and skills to improve numerical literacy are discussed.

Chapter 6

Summary and conclusion

The book has considered several types of disability and disorder:

- Reading disorder
- Disorder of written expression
- Developmental co-ordination disorder
- Mathematics disorder.

For each disorder it was maintained that there are particular implications for provision. This was considered in terms of:

- The curriculum and related assessment
- Pedagogy
- Resources
- School and classroom organisation
- Therapy and care.

Reading disorder

I looked at definitions of reading disorder; its prevalence; some character-istics of reading difficulties; causal factors; and identification and assessment. I considered possible associated difficulties, their assessment and related provision. These were phonological difficulties, visual processing diffi-culties, auditory perception and auditory processing difficulties, short term verbal memory difficulties, and sequencing difficulties of temporal order.

I looked at provision for reading and for reading skills. These were direct code instruction, phonological training, combination training, and assisting the generalisation of phonological skills to reading. The chapter also considered provision for reading fluency and reading com-prehension. I examined alternative and augmentative communication.

The final section summarised provision in relation to curriculum and assessment; pedagogy; resources; therapy/care; and school and classroom organisation.

Disorder of written expression

This chapter looked at a definition of disorder of written expression, prevalence, causal factors, and identification and assessment. I distinguished between traditional and process based approaches to teaching writing. In provision for writing and spelling, I examined remediating sequencing, improving co-ordination skills for handwriting, and teaching cursive script.

Regarding provision for writing composition, I looked at frameworks for writing, reducing task demands, software for essay structure, note taking, writing for a purpose, and developing self-regulation strategies. For spelling, I considered: multi-sensory aspects, Directed Spelling Thinking Activity, and target words. The chapter considered alternative and augmentative communication including the use of symbols. I summarised provision in terms of curriculum and assessment; pedagogy; resources; therapy/care; and organisation.

Developmental co-ordination disorder

This chapter provided a definition of developmental co-ordination disorder and looked at estimates of its prevalence. I considered possible causal factors. The chapter examines developmental processes considered to underpin developmental co-ordination disorder. These were identified as gross and fine motor co-ordination, and perceptual-motor development.

I looked at ways of assessing developmental co-ordination disorder. Turning to provision, the chapter outlined aspects of the curriculum; pedagogy; resources; therapy/care and organisation. Under pedagogy, the chapter examined approaches to handwriting, physical education, and personal and social development. Care and therapy discussed the approach of Cognitive Orientation to Daily Occupational Performance.

Mathematics disorder

This chapter considered definitions of mathematics disorder; its prevalence; causal factors; and its identification and assessment. I described provision in relation to teaching prerequisite skills (classification, number, length, area, volume, weight, position, and movement). The chapter examined general approaches (reducing anxiety, concrete experience, adapting and applying knowledge and mathematical problem solving). I looked at mathematics difficulties relating to developmental co-ordination disorder (number; shape, space and measure).

I considered mathematics difficulties relating to reading disorder (phonological difficulties and auditory perception and auditory processing difficulties, difficulty with working memory, sequencing difficulties). I summarised provision with regard to curriculum and assessment; pedagogy; resources; therapy/care; and school and classroom organisation.

A final word

The above summary of provision for different types of disability and disorder that have been examined in this book indicates the importance to schools of reviewing their curriculum, pedagogy, resources, organisation and therapy. In doing so the school will be able to ensure that provision helps encourage the best academic progress and the best personal and social development for its pupils.

Another essential aspect of special education that has been implicit throughout the book is that of professionals working closely with parents and other professionals. It is helpful to recognise the importance of professional contributions and the foundational disciplines that contribute to special education. Examples of these foundational disciplines are:

- Legal/typological
- Terminological
- Social
- Medical
- Neuropsychological
- Psychotherapeutic
- Behavioural/observational
- Developmental
- Psycholinguistic
- Technological
- Pedagogical.

Legal/typological foundations of special education concern social, political and economic factors informing the context of special education legislation. It includes an understanding of current legislation and the main types of disabilities and disorders drawing on classifications used in the systems in the country concerned. Terminological matters include the importance of terminology in special education; for example: 'needs', 'discrimination' and 'rights'. Social foundations include a social constructionist perspective. A social view of disability has been important in widening the understanding beyond individual factors. Medical influences involve the scope of the application of medical perspectives and the use of drugs in relation to children with disabilities and disorders.

Neuropsychological aspects draw on techniques used in neurological research and some uses of psychological and related tests in neuropsychology. Psychotherapeutic contributions involve systems, psychodynamic and cognitive-behavioural approaches. Behavioural and observational foundations consider behavioural approaches to learning with reference to learning theory and observational learning and modelling in social cognitive theory. Developmental features may draw on Piaget's theory of genetic epistemology for example in relation to understandings of provision for children with cognitive impairment.

Psycholinguistic foundations involve frameworks incorporating input processing, lexical representations, and output processing, as well as interventions. Technological aspects may explore how technology constitutes a foundation of special education through its enhancement of teaching and learning. Pedagogical aspects examine pedagogy in relation to special education, in particular the issue of distinctive pedagogy for different types of disabilities and disorders.

The book, *Foundations of Special Education: An introduction* (Farrell, 2009a) discusses these areas in detail.

Bibliography

Addy, L. M. (2004) *Speed Up! A Kinaesthetic Approach to Handwriting* Cambridge, LDA Ltd.

Ahonen, T., Kooistra, L., Viholainen, H. and Cantell, M. (2004) 'Developmental Motor Learning Disability: A Neuropsychological Approach' in Dewey, D. and Tupper, D. E. (Eds.) *Developmental Motor Disorders: A Neuropsychological Perspective* New York, Guilford Press

American Psychiatric Association (2000) *Diagnostic and Statistical Manual of Mental Disorders Fourth Edition Text Revision* Washington DC, American Psychiatric Association

Ayres, A. J. (1989) *Sensory integration and praxis tests* Los Angeles, CA, Western Psychological Services

Ayers, H. and Prytys, C. (2002) *An A to Z Practical Guide to Emotional and Behavioural Difficulties* London, David Fulton Publishers.

Battista, M.T. (1999) 'The mathematical miseducation of America's youth: ignoring research and scientific study in education' *Phi Delta Kappan* 80, 6, 425–33

Beaton, A. A. (2004) *Dyslexia, Reading and the Brain: A Sourcebook of Biological and Psychological Research* London, Psychology Press

Beitchman, J. H. and Young, A. R. (1997) 'Learning disorders with a special emphasis on reading disorders: A review of the past ten years' *Journal of the American Academy of Child and Adolescent Psychiatry* 40, 75–82

Benbow, M. (1990) *Loops and other groups: A kinaesthetic writing system* Tucson, AZ, Therapy Skill Builders

——(2002) 'Hand skills and Handwriting' in Cermak, S. A. and Larkin, D. (2002) *Developmental Coordination Disorder* (pp. 248 – 279) Albany, New York, Delmar Thompson Learning

Berch, D. B. (2005) 'Making sense of number sense: Implications for Children with mathematical disabilities' *Journal of Learning Disabilities* 38, 333–39

Berninger, V. W. (1994) 'Future directions for research on writing disabilities: Integrating endogenous and exogenous variables' In Lyon, G. R. (Ed.) *Frames of reference for the assessment of learning disabilities* (pp. 419–40) Baltimore, Brookes

Berninger, V. W. and Amtmann, D. (2003) 'Preventing written expression disabilities through early intervention and continuing assessment and intervention for handwriting and/or spelling problems: Research into practice' (chapter 23) in

Swanson, H. L., Harris, K. R. and Graham, S. (Eds.) (2003) *Handbook of Learning Disabilities* New York, NY, Guilford Press

Bigge, J. L., Best, S. J. and Heller, K. W. (2001) (4th. edition) *Teaching Individuals with Physical, Health or Multiple Disabilities* Upper Saddle River, NJ, Merrill-Prentice Hall

Black, K. and Haskins, D. (1996) 'Including all children in TOP PLAY and BT TOP SPORT' *British Journal of Physical Education*, Primary PE Focus, Winter edition 9, 11

Brooks, G. (2002) *What Works for Reading Difficulties? The Effectiveness of Intervention Schemes* London, Department of Education and Science

Bundy, A. (2002) 'Play in children with DCD: what we know and what we suspect,' 5th Biennial conference on Developmental Co-ordination Disorders Bannf, Alberter, Canada

Butterworth, B. (2004) *Dyscalculia Screener* Swindon, NFER-Nelson

Campbell, J. (Ed.) (2005) *Handbook of Mathematical Cognition* New York, Taylor and Francis

Cawley, J., Parmar, R., Foley, T., Salmon, S. and Roy, S. (2001) 'Arithmetic performance of students: implications for standards and programming' *Exceptional Children* 67, 3, 311–328

Cermak, S. A. and Larkin, D. (2002) *Developmental Coordination Disorder* Albany, New York, Delmar Thompson Learning

Cermak, S. A. Gubbay, S. S. and Larkin, D. (2002) 'What is developmental co-ordination disorder?' In Cermak, S. A. and Larkin, D. (eds.) *Developmental Co-ordination Disorder* Albany, NY, Delmar

Chinn, S. and Ashcroft, R. (2006) (3rd. edition) *Mathematics for Dyslexics, Including Dyscalculia* London, Wiley

Clough, C. (1999) *Teaching cursive writing* OT Practice 4, 8, 41–42

Corkin, S. (1974) 'Serial order deficits in inferior readers' *Neuropsychologia* 12, 347–54

Crawford, S. G., Wilson, B. N. and Dewey, D. (2001) 'Identifying developmental co-ordination disorder: consistency between tests' in *Children with Developmental Co-ordination Disorder: Strategies for Success* Binghamton, NY, Hawthorne Press

Dean, E., Howell, J. and Waters, D. (1990) *Metaphon Resource Pack* Windsor, NFER-Nelson

Dehaene, S., Dehaene-Lambertz, G. and Cohen, L. (1998) 'Abstract representations of numbers in the animal and human brain' *Trends in Neuroscience* 21, 8, 355–61

De La Paz, S., Swanson, P. and Graham, S. (1998) 'The contribution of executive control to the revising of students with writing and learning difficulties' *Journal of Educational Psychology* 90, 448–60

Department of Education and Skills (2001a) *The National Numeracy Strategy Guidance to Support Pupils with Dyslexia and Dyscalculia* London, DfES

——(2001b) *Special Educational Needs Code of Practice* London, DfES

——(2005) (2nd. Edition) *Data Collection by Special Educational Need* London, DfES

Dewey, D. and Wilson, B. N. (2001) 'Developmental Coordination Disorder: What is it?' in Missiuna, C. (Ed.) *Children with Developmental Disorder: Strategies for Success* New York, The Haworth Press (pp. 51–68)

Dixon, G. and Addy, L. M. (2004) *Making Inclusion Work for Children with Dyspraxia: Practical Strategies for Teachers* London, Routledge-Falmer

Dowker, A. (2005) *Individual Differences in Arithmetic: Implications for Psychology, Neuroscience and Education* New York, Taylor and Francis

Dykman, R. A. and Ackerman, P. T. (1992) 'Diagnosing dyslexia: IQ regression plus cut points' *Journal of Learning Disabilities* 25, 574–76

El-Nagar, O. (1996) *Specific Learning Difficulties in Mathematics: A Classroom Approach* Tamworth, National Association of Special Educational Needs

Estil, L. and Whiting, H. T. A. (2002) 'Motor/Language Impairment Syndromes – Direct or Indirect Foundations' in Cermak, S. A. and Larkin, D. (2002) *Developmental Coordination Disorder* Albany, New York, Delmar Thompson Learning

Farrell, M. (2009a), *Foundations of Special Education: An Introduction* Oxford, United Kingdom and Malden MA, Wiley-Blackwell

——(2009b) (4th. edition) *The Special Education Handbook*, London, David Fulton Publishers

——(2010) (2nd. Edition) *The Effective Teacher's Guide to Sensory and Physical Impairments: Sensory, Orthopaedic, Motor and Health Impairments, and Traumatic Brain Injury* New York, NY and London, Routledge

——(2010) (2nd. Edition) *The Effective Teacher's Guide to Behavioural and Emotional Disorders: Disruptive behaviour disorders, anxiety disorders and depressive disorders, and attention deficit hyperactivity disorder* New York, NY and London, Routledge

——(2011) (2nd. Edition) *The Effective Teacher's Guide to Autism and Communication Difficulties* (2nd. Edition) New York, NY and London, Routledge

——(2011) (2nd. Edition) *The Effective Teacher's Guide to Learning Disorders* New York, NY and London, Routledge

——(2011) (2nd. Edition) *The Effective Teacher's Guide to Cognitive Impairments* (2nd. Edition) New York, NY and London, Routledge

——(2009) (4th. edition) *The Special Education Handbook* London, David Fulton

Fisher, S. E. and DeFries, J. C. (2002) 'Developmental dyslexia: Genetic dissection of a complex cognitive trait' *Nature Reviews*, Neuroscience 3, 10, 767–80

Fleischner, J. E. and Manheimer, M. A. (1997) 'Math intervention for students with learning disabilities: myths and realities' *School Psychology Review* 26, 3, 397–413

Fletcher, J. M., Lyon, G. R., Fuchs, L. and Barnes, M. A. (2007) *Learning Disabilities: From Identification to Intervention* New York, Guilford Press

Fonagy, P., Target, M., Cottrell, D., Phillips, J. and Kurtz, Z. (2005) *What Works for Whom? A Critical Review of Treatments for Children and Adolescents* New York, Guilford Press

Foorman, B. R., Francis, D. J., Fletcher, J. M., Schatschneider, C. and Mehta, P. (1998) 'The role of instruction in learning to read: Preventing reading failure in at risk children' *Journal of Educational Psychology* 90, 1, 37–55

Fuchs, L. S. and Fuchs, D. (2003) 'Enhancing the mathematical Problem Solving of Students with Mathematics Disabilities' in Swanson, H. L., Harris, K. R. and Graham, S. (Eds.) (2003) *Handbook of Learning Disabilities* New York, Guilford Press

Gabbard, C. LeBlanc, B. and Lowry, S. (1994) (2nd. Edition) *Physical education for children: Building the foundation* Upper Saddle River NJ, Prentice-Hall

Geary, D. C. (2003) 'Learning Disabilities in Arithmetic: Problem Solving Differences and Cognitive Deficits' in Swanson, H. L., Harris, K. R. and Graham, S. (Eds.) (2003) *Handbook of Learning Disabilities* New York, Guilford Press (pp. 199–212).

Geary, D. C., Hamson, C. O. and Hoard, M. K. (2000) 'Numerical and arithmetical cognition: A longitudinal study of process and concept deficits in children with learning disability' *Journal of Experimental Child Psychology* 77, 236–63

Geary, D. C. and Hoard, M. K. (2001) 'Numerical and arithmatical deficits in learning disabled children: Relation to dyscalculia and dyslexia' *Aphasiology* 15, 7, 635–647.

Gersten, R., Fuchs, L. S., Williams, J. P. and Baker, S. (2001) 'Teaching reading comprehension strategies to students with learning disabilities: A review of research' *Review of Educational Research* 71, 279–320

Gersten, R., Chard, D., Baker, S. Jayanthi, N., Flojo, J. and Lee, D. (under review) 'Experimental and quasi-experimental research on instructional approaches for teaching mathematics to students with learning disabilities. A research synthesis' *Review of Educational Research*

Gillberg, C. (1996) *Ett barn I varje klass. Om DAMP, MBD, ADHD* Södertälje, Cura

Godfrey J. J., Syrdal-Lasky, A. K., Millay, K. *et al.* (1981) 'Performance of dyslexic children on speech perception tests' *Journal of Experimental Child Psychology* 32, 401–24

Goswami, U. (2004) 'Neuroscience, education and special education' *British Journal of Special Education* 31, 4, 175–83

Graham, S. (1990) 'The role of production factors in learning disabled students compositions' *Journal of Educational Psychology* 82, 781–91

——(2000) 'Should the natural learning approach replace spelling instruction?' *Journal of Educational Psychology* 92, 2, 235–47

Graham, S., Harris, K. and Loynachan, C. (2000) 'The Directed Spelling Thinking Activity: application with high frequency words' *Learning Disabilities: Research and Practice* 11, 1, 34–40

Graham, S., Harris, K. R., McArthur, C. and Schwartz, S. (1991) 'Writing and writing instruction with students with learning disabilities: A review of a program of research' *Learning Disability Quarterly* 14, 89–114

Graham, S. and Harris, K. R. (1997) 'Self-regulation and writing: Where do we go from here?' *Contemporary Educational Psychology* 22, 102–14

——(2003) 'Students with Learning Disabilities and the Process of Writing: A Meta-analysis of SRDS Studies' in Swanson, H. L., Harris, K. R. and Graham, S. (Eds.) (2003) *Handbook of Learning Disabilities* New York, Guilford Press (pp. 323–44)

Gregg, N. and Mather, N. (2002) 'School is fun at recess: Informal analyses of written language for students with learning disabilities' *Journal of Learning Disabilities* 35, 1, 7–22

Gubbay, S. S. (1985) 'Clumsiness' in Vinken, P., Bruyn, G. and Klawans, H. (Eds.) *Handbook of Clinical Neurology Vol. 2 (46) Neurobehavioral Disorders* (pp. 159 – 167) New York, Elsevier Science

Gunning, T. G. (2002) (2nd. Edition) *Assessing and Correcting Reading and Writing Difficulties* Boston, MA, Allyn and Bacon

Hagtvet, B. E. (1997) 'Phonological and linguistic-cognitive precursors of reading abilities' *Dyslexia* 3,3

Harwayne, S. (2001) *Writing Through Childhood* Portsmouth, NH, Heinemann

Hatcher, P. (2000) 'Sound links in reading and spelling with discrepancy defined dyslexics and children with moderate learning difficulties' *Reading and Writing: An Interdisciplinary Journal* 13, 257–72

Hess, M. and Wheldall, K. (1999) 'Strategies for improving the written expression of primary children with poor writing skills' *Australian Journal of Learning Disabilities* 4, 4, 14–20

Hoare, D. (1994) 'Subtypes of developmental coordination disorder' *Adapted Physical Activity Quarterly* 11, 158–69

Howell, J. and Dean, E. (1994) (2nd. Edition) *Treating Phonological Disorders in Children – Metaphon – Theory to Practice* London, Whurr Publishers.

Hulme, C. and Snowling, M. (1997) *Dyslexia: Biology, Cognition and Intervention* London, Whurr Publishers

Hynd, G. W., Semrud-Clikeman, M., Lorys, A., Novey, E. and Eliopulos, D. (1990) 'Brain morphology in developmental dyslexia and attention deficit hyperactivity disorder' *Archives of Neurology* 47, 919–26

Irlen, H. L. (1994) 'Scotopic sensitivity: Irlen syndrome hypothesis and explanation of the syndrome' *Journal of Behavioural Optometry* 5, 65–66

Jordan, N. C. and Hanich, L. B. (2003) 'Characteristics of Children with Moderate Mathematics Deficiencies: A Longitudinal Perspective' *Learning Disabilities Research* and Practice 18, 4, 213–21

Jordan, N. C., Hanich, L. B. and Kaplan, D. (2003) 'A Longitudinal Study of Mathematical Competencies in Children with Specific Mathematics Difficulties Versus Children with Comorbid Mathematics and Reading Difficulties' *Child Development* 74, 3, 834–50

Kaplan, B. J., Wilson, B. N., Dewey, D. and Crawford, S. G. (1998) 'DCD may not be a discrete disorder' *Journal of Human Movement Science* 17, 471–90

Kauffman, J. M. and Hallahan, D. P. (2005) *Special Education: What It Is and Why We Need It* Boston, MA, Pearson/Allyn and Bacon

Kavale, K. and Mattson, D. (1983) ' "One jumped off the balance beam": a meta-analysis of perceptual-motor training' *Journal of Learning Disabilities* 16, 3, 165–73

Kavale, K. A. and Forness, S. R. (1995) *The nature of learning disabilities: Critical elements in diagnosis and classification* Mahwah, NJ, Erlbaum

Kirby, A. and Drew, S. (2003) *Guide to Dyspraxia and Developmental Co-ordination Disorders* London, David Fulton Publishers.

Klingner, J., Vaughn, S. and Boardman A. (2007) *Teaching Reading Comprehension to Students with Learning Difficulties* New York, Guilford Press

Kopera-Frye, K., Dahaene, S. and Streissguth, A. P. (1996) 'Impairments of number processing induced by prenatal alcohol exposure' *Neuropsychologia* 34, 1187–96

Landgren, M., Kjellman, B. and Gillberg, C. (1998) 'Attention deficit disorder with developmental coordination disorders' *Archives of Disease in Childhood* 79, 3, 207–12

Laszlo, J. I. and Bairstow, P. J. (1985) *Perceptual-motor behaviour: developmental assessment and therapy* New York, NY, Praeger

Lewis, R., Graves, A., Ashton, T. and Kieley, C. (1998) 'Word processing tools for students with learning disabilities: A comparison of strategies to increase text entry speed' *Learning Disabilities Research and Practice* 13, 95–108

Lovett, M. W., Lacerenza, L., Borden, S. L. (2000) 'Putting struggling readers on the PHAST track: A program to integrate phonological and strategy based remedial reading instruction and maximise outcomes' *Journal of Learning Disabilities* 33, 5, 458–76

Lovett, M. W., Lacerenza, L., Borden, S. L., Frijters, J. C., Steinbach, K. A. and De Palma, M. (2000) 'Components of effective remediation for developmental reading disabilities: Combining phonological and strategy-based instruction to improve outcomes' *Journal of Educational Psychology* 92, 2, 263–83

Lovett, M. W., Steinbach, K. A. and Frijters, J. C. (2000) 'Remediating the core deficits of developmental reading disability: A double deficit perspective' *Journal of Learning Disabilities* 33, 4, 334–58

McDougal, S. J., Hulme, C., Ellis, A. *et al.*, (1994) 'Learning to read: the role of short-term memory and phonological skills' *Journal of Experimental Child Psychology* 58, 112–33

Macintyre, C. and Deponio, P. (2003) *Identifying and supporting children with specific learning difficulties: Looking beyond the label to assess the whole child* New York, Routledge Falmer

Mandich, A. D., Polatajko, H. J., Macnab, J. J. and Miller, L. T. (2001) 'Treatment of Children with developmental Coordination Disorder: What is the Evidence?' in Missiuna, C. (Ed.) *Children with Developmental Co-ordination Disorder: Strategies for success* New York, Haworth Press

Martin, D. and Miller, C. (2003) *Speech and Language Difficulties in the Classroom* London, David Fulton Publishers

Martini, R., Heath, N. and Missiuna, C. (1999) 'A North American analysis of the relationship between learning disabilities and developmental coordination disorder' *International Journal of Learning Disabilities* 14, 46–58

May-Benson, T., Ingolia, P. and Koomar, J. (2002) 'Daily Living Skills and Developmental Coordination Disorder' in Cermak, S. A. and Larkin, D. (2002) *Developmental Coordination Disorder* Albany, New York, Delmar Thompson Learning

Mercer, C. D. and Mercer, A. R. (1998) *Teaching students with learning problems* New York, Merrill

Miles, T. R. and Miles, E. (1990) *Dyslexia: A Hundred Years On* Buckingham, Open University Press

Missiuna, C. (Ed.) (2001) *Children with Developmental Co-ordination Disorder: Strategies for success* New York, Haworth Press

Morrow, L. M. (2001) (4th. edition) *Literacy Development in the Early Years: Helping Children Read and Write* Boston, MA, Allyn and Bacon

Nelson, N. and Calfee, R. C. (1998) *The Reading-Writing Connection* Chicago, IL, National Society for the Study of Education

Ostad, S. A. (1999) 'Developmental progression of subtraction strategies: a comparison of mathematically normal and mathematically disabled children' *European Journal of Special Needs Education* 14, 1, 21–36

Palmer, S. (2000) 'Phonological recoding deficit in working memory of dyslexic teenager' *Journal of Research in Reading* 23, 28–40

Paulesu, E., Demonet, J. F., Fazio, F., McCrory, E., Chanoine, V., Brunswick, N., Cappa, S., Cossu, G., Habib, M., Frith, C. and Frith, U. (2001) 'Dyslexia – Cultural diversity and biological unity' *Science* 291, 2165–67

Polatajko, H. J., Mandich, A. D, Miller, L. T. and Macnab, J. J. (2001) 'Cognitive orientation to daily occupational performance (CO-OP): Part II – The evidence' *Physical and Occupational Therapy in Paediatrics* 20, 2/3, 83 – 106

Polatajko, H., Mandich, A., Missuina, C., Miller, L., Macnab, J., Malloy-Miller, T. et al., (2001) 'Cognitive orientation to daily occupational performance (CO-OP): Part III – The protocol in brief' *Physical and Occupational Therapy in Paediatrics* 20, 107 – 123

Polatajko, H. and Mandich, A. (2004) *Enabling occupation in children: The Cognitive Orientation to Daily Occupational Performance (CO-OP) approach* Ottawa, CAOT Publications

Polatajko, H. J., Rodger, S., Dhillon, A. and Hirji, F. (2004) 'Approaches to the Management of Children with Motor Problems' in Dewey, D. and Tupper, D. (Eds.) (2004) *Developmental Motor Disorders: A Neuropsychological Perspective* New York, Guilford Press

Pollington, M. F., Wilcox, B. and Morrison, T. G. (2001) 'Self-perception in writing: the effects of writing workshop and traditional instruction on intermediate grade students' *Reading Psychology* 22, 249–65

Pollock, J., Waller, E. and Pollitt, R. (2004) (2nd. Edition) *Day-to-Day Dyslexia in the Classroom* London, Routledge Falmer

Poustie, J. (2001a) *Mathematics Solutions: An Introduction to Dyscalculia Part A – How to Identify, Assess and Manage Specific Learning Difficulties in Mathematics* Taunton, Next Generation

——(2001b) *Mathematics Solutions: An Introduction to Dyscalculia Part B – How to Teach Children and Adults who have Specific Learning Difficulties in Mathematics* Taunton, Next Generation

Pryde, K. M. (2000) *Sensorimotor functioning in developmental co-ordination disorder: A kinaesthetic and psychometric analysis*, unpublished doctoral dissertation: University of Waterloo, Waterloo, Ontario, Canada

Revie, G. and Larkin, D. (1993) 'Task-specific intervention with children reduces movement problems' *Adapt. Phys. Activ. Quarterly* 10, 29–41

Reynolds, C. R. and Fletcher-Janzen, E. (Eds.) (2004) (2nd. Edition) *Concise Encyclopaedia of Special Education: A Reference for the Education of Handicapped and Other Exceptional Children and Adults* Hoboken, NY, John Wiley and Sons

Rosen, G. D. (2006) *The Dyslexic Brain: New Pathways in Neuroscience Discovery* New York, Taylor and Francis

Roy, E. A., Bottos, S., Pryde, K. and Dewey, D. (2004) 'Approaches to Understanding the Neurobehavioral Mechanisms Associated with Motor Impairment in Children' in Dewey, D. and Tupper, D. E. (Eds.) *Developmental Disorders: A Neurological Perspective* New York, Guilford Press

Sandler, A. D., Watson, T. E., Footo, M., Levine, M. D., Coleman, W. L. and Hooper, S. R. (1992) 'Neurodevelopmental study of writing disorders in middle childhood' *Journal of Developmental and Behavioural Paediatrics* 13, 17–23

Sexton, R. J., Harris, K. R. and Graham, S. (1998) 'The effects of self regulated strategy development on essay writing and attributions of students with learning disabilities in a process writing setting' *Exceptional Children* 64, 295–311

Share, D. L. (1995) 'Phonological recoding and self teaching: sine qua non of reading acquisition' *Cognition* 55, 151–218

Silver, A. A. and Hagin, R. A. (2002) (2nd. Edition) *Disorders of Learning in Childhood* New York, Wiley.

Snowling, M. J. (2000) *Dyslexia* Oxford, Blackwell

Standring, S. (39th. Edition) (2005) *Gray's Anatomy: The Anatomical Basis of Clinical Practice* London, Elsevier Churchill Livingstone

Stanovich, K. (1994) 'Annotation: Does dyslexia exist?' *Journal of Child Psychology and Psychiatry* 35, 4, 579–95

Stein, J. F. (1995) 'A visual deficit in dyslexia?' in Nicholson, R. I. and Fawcett, A. J. (Eds.) *Dyslexia in Children: Multidisciplinary Perspectives* Hemel Hempstead, Harvester Wheatsheaf

Stein, J. F., Talcott, J. and Witton, C. (2001) 'Dyslexia: the role of the magnocellular system', paper presented at the 5th. British Dyslexia Association Conference

Sugden, D. and Chambers, M. (2005) *Children with Developmental Coordination Disorder* London, Wiley

Swanson, H. L. and Hoskyn, M. (1998) 'Experimental intervention research on students with learning disabilities: A meta-analysis of treatment outcomes' *Review of Educational Research* 68, 3, 277–321

Swanson, H. L., Harris, K. R. and Graham, S. (Eds.) (2003) *Handbook of Learning Disabilities* New York, Guilford Press

Taylor, M. B. and Williams, J. P. (1983) 'Comprehension of LD readers: Task and text variations' *Journal of Educational Psychology* 75, 743–51

Tiedt, P. L. Tiedt, I. M. and Tiedt, S. W. (2001) (3rd. edition) *Language Arts Activities for the Classroom* Boston, MA, Allyn and Bacon

Torgesen, J. K. (2000) 'Individual differences in response to early interventions in reading: The lingering problem of treatment registers' *Learning Disabilities Research and Practice* 15, 1, 55–64

Torgesen, J. K. and Mathes, P. G. (2000) *A Basic Guide to Understanding, Assessing and Teaching Phonological Awareness* Austin, TX, ProEd

Vanderheiden, G. C. and Lloyd, L. L. (1986) 'Communication systems and their components' in Blackstone, S. W. Bruskin, D. M. (Eds.) *Augmentative Communication: An Introduction* Rockville, MD, American Speech-Language-Hearing Association (pp. 29–162)

Westwood, P. (2000) *Numeracy and Learning Difficulties: Approaches to Teaching and Assessment* London, David Fulton Publishers.

——(2003) (4th. edition) *Commonsense Methods for Children with Special Educational Needs: Strategies for the Regular Classroom* London, Routledge Falmer

Williams, J. P. (2003) 'Teaching Text Structure to Improve reading Comprehension' in Swanson, H. L., Harris, K. R. and Graham, S. (Eds.) (2003) *Handbook of Learning Disabilities* New York, Guilford Press (pp. 293–305).

Williams, J. P., Taylor, M. B., Jarin, D. C. and Milligan, E. S. (1983) *Determining the main idea of expository paragraphs: An instructional program for the learning disabled and its evaluation* (Technical Report #25) Research Institute for the Study of Learning Disabilities Teachers College, Columbia University

Wilson, P. H. and McKenzie, B. E. (1998) 'Information processing deficits associated with Developmental Coordination Disorder: A meta-analysis of research findings' *Journal of Child Psychology and Allied Disciplines* 39, 829–40

Wilson, B. M. and Proctor, A. (2000) 'Oral and written discourse in adolescents with closed head injury' *Brain and Cognition* 43, 425–29

Wilson, P. (2005) 'Visuospatial, Kinesthetic, Visuomotor Integration, and Visuo-constructional Disorders: Implications for Motor development' in Dewey, D. and Tupper, D. E. (Eds.) *Developmental Disorders: A Neurological Perspective* New York, Guilford Press

Wise, B. W., Ring, J. and Olsen, R. K. (2000) 'Individual differences in gains from computer assisted remedial reading' *Journal of Experimental Psychology* 77, 197–235

Wolf, M., Miller, L. and Donnelly, K. (2000) 'Retrieval, automaticity, vocabulary elaboration, orthography (RAVE-O): A comprehensive, fluency-based reading intervention program' *Journal of Learning Disabilities* 33, 4, 375–86

Wolf, M. and O'Brien, B. (2001) 'On issues of time, fluency and intervention' in Fawcett, A. (Ed.) *Dyslexia: Theory and Good Practice* London, Whurr Publishers

Wong, B. Y. L. (1991) 'On cognitive process-based instruction: an introduction', *Journal of Learning Disabilities* 25, 3, 150–52, 172

Zago, L., Presenti, M., Mellet, E. *et al.* (2001) 'Neural correlates of simple and complex mental calculation' *Neuroimage* 13, 314–27

Zutell, J. (1998) 'Word sorting: a developmental approach to word study for delayed readers' *Reading and Writing Quarterly* 14, 219–38

Index